LOBBY CARDS

SAVANNAH THEATRE, Savannah, Georgia
Said to be the oldest continuously-operated theatre in the United States.

LOBBY CARDS

THE MICHAEL HAWKS COLLECTION · VOLUME II

Foreword by Bob Hope

Text by Kathryn Leigh Scott

Pomegranate Press, Ltd. · *Los Angeles* · *London*

This is a Pomegranate Press, Ltd. book

Copyright © 1988 by Pomegranate Press, Ltd.
First Printing 1988

The Library of Congress Catalog Card Number is 88-061065

ISBN: 0-938817-13-2

NOTES ON THE COMPOSITION
Book Jacket Design: Tony Gleeson
Book Design: Tony Gleeson
Photographic Reproduction: Ben Martin
Photographic Assistant: Byron Cohen
Research: Kathleen Resch

The text was typeset in Schneidler by Marchese Graphics Incorporated, Los Angeles;
and was printed and bound in Japan by Dai Nippon Printing Co., Ltd., Tokyo, Japan.

ACKNOWLEDGEMENTS

For their special contributions, we wish to thank A + I Photo Lab; Timothy Burke, Hollywood Studio Museum; Leroy Chen; Smae Spaulding Davis; Gwen Feldman; Harry and Pam Flynn; Patricia Gibson; Kyo Il and Mi Ja Hwang, Hollywood Photo Lab; Mark Jacobsen, Jacobsen Photographic Instruments; Carol Judy Leslie; Gil and Miranda Lipton; Leonard Maltin; Melinda Manos; Kohei Tsumori, Dai Nippon Printing (America); and Marc Wanamaker/Bison Archives. Sincere appreciation to the staff of the Margaret Herrick Library at the Academy of Motion Picture Arts and Sciences and Academy Foundation, and to all the film studios for their generous help and cooperation.

CONTENTS

FOREWORD

Looking through these lobby cards brings back some great memories. When I was a youngster, we'd hang around the nickelodeons figuring out how to scare up the few pennies to get inside — meanwhile staring enthralled at lobby cards of the crazy Keystone Kops and the daredevil comics dangling off cliffs in old jalopies. We'd itch to get inside to see the antics of great talents like Chaplin and Keaton. Who could forget it?

And how these memories come alive in this beautiful book. Thanks to Michael Hawks — who has collected over 4,000 of these great cards — this theatrical memorabilia has been preserved for future generations of movie buffs. Kathryn Leigh Scott has added spice to the pot with her tasty anecdotes, and together they've assembled a feast of film lore you can sink your teeth into.

The first card in the book — Charlie Chaplin in THE FIREMAN (1916) — trips the memory box right away. As a kid in Cleveland, I first broke into show business doing Chaplin imitations in a Little Tramp look-alike contest. How long ago was that? Seems like yesterday.

The next three cards feature Roscoe Arbuckle, a big star of the '20s who fell on hard times. I met "Fatty" at the Bandbox in Cleveland when he was making a comeback in a little revue. At that time I was a vaudeville hoofer in "tab" shows — short for tabloid musical comedy — doing soft-shoe, tap and buck-and-wing. Arbuckle set me up with "Hurley's Jolly Follies" and because of him I graduated to comic routines.

Thanks to this book, I'm reminded of a lot of comedians who were big in their time and are now largely forgotten. We all remember Lloyd, Keaton and Chaplin, but the limelight faded long ago on Harry Langdon, Max Linder, Raymond Griffith and Charley Chase. A lot of the comedy routines you see in films today are inspired by the gags originated by these pioneers in the old two-reelers. And where'd they come from? Those performers spent years on the road developing their acts in traveling medicine shows, music halls, the circus — and, of course, vaudeville.

Vaudeville spawned a lot of wonderful comic talents who moved into pictures, and they're all here — W. C. Fields, Ruby Keeler, Fanny Brice, Eddie Cantor, Burns and Allen, Jimmy Durante, Ethel Merman — and yes, Bing Crosby. Seeing the card for one of my early shorts, WATCH THE BIRDIE, reminds me that Bing and I were first on screen together in a short called DON'T HOOK NOW. And wouldn't ya know? It's about golf.

The card for INTERNATIONAL HOUSE (1933) reminds me of my introduction to features a few years later in THE BIG BROADCAST OF 1938 — in a role Jack Benny was too busy to do. A picture like that was called a "clambake." Just about every Paramount contract player was in it — including Dorothy Lamour, a luscious songbird I first met in New York. She soon joined Bing and me in our first "road" picture, THE ROAD TO SINGAPORE. If this lobby card could only talk. What a time we had! The whole idea, according to writer Don Hartman, was "You take a piece of used chewing gum and flip it at a map. Wherever it sticks you can lay a "road" picture, so long as the people there are jokers who cook and eat strangers." And take a look at that camel in THE ROAD TO MOROCCO card. As I walked up, that scene-stealing dromedary turned and spit in my eye. "PRINT THAT!" the director shouted — and it's in the film. We did seven "road" pictures and two of them are included in this collection.

This book is full of memories for me. I've crossed paths onscreen and off — and shared a lot of gags — with most of the folks pictured here. It's been a lot of fun.

Hey, thanks for the memories.

Bob Hope

The Michael Hawks Collection

It's a hot, dry, typically sunny Southern California day, and the last day of a long holiday weekend. I wind through the quiet streets of my Hollywood neighborhood and soon join the throngs on the freeway heading toward the beach. But there's no surfboard strapped to the roof of my car and I'm not cruising to Malibu to fry my skin on the sandy shores of the Pacific. Instead, with a week left before this book goes to press, I'm taking the day off to join a dozen other movie fanatics in a friend's darkened living room to watch a marathon of Our Gang shorts. It's my idea of a good time, and a great way to avoid sunburn.

Not long ago I read that most people who ask for a particular title in a video store are seeking a vintage movie, and that most of the old classics requested aren't available on cassette. That's been my experience, too. Early films starring long forgotten stars of the silent era are difficult to find even in university film libraries, and are rarely included in museum or art house revivals. But, just as I collect lobby cards, I have friends who stock their private film libraries with reels of rare old movies and genre favorites — for example, Republic westerns and serials, the Three Stooges, film noir/detective movies or science fiction/horror films.

Leaving the beach traffic, I turn off the freeway and drive toward the foothills of the valley to the home of a friend who has specialized in collecting more than a thousand vintage comedies, including much of director Leo McCarey's work in mid-'20s short subjects and actor Lloyd Hamilton's early sound films. His kitchen doubles as a projection room, enabling him to screen 16mm and 35mm prints in his living room. Some years ago he found a badly damaged machine in a derelict Canadian theatre and recognized it as a Fotoplayer, a musical instrument of the '20s frequently found in the nickelodeons of the day. Resembling a typical player piano with a keyboard, the instrument is also fitted with a device containing various implements that enable it to produce sound effects: thunder, drums, whistles, breaking china, fire alarms, horses' hooves and screeching trains. Fully restored, it's the perfect accompaniment to

AMBROSE'S RAPID RISE
1916 Triangle • Keystone
STARRING: Mack Swain,
               Louella Maxam,
               Tom Kennedy,
               Robert Kortman
DIRECTOR: Fred Fishback
PICTURED: Louella Maxam,
               Tom Kennedy,
               Mack Swain

CROOKED TO THE END
1915 Triangle • Keystone
STARRING: Fred Mace,
               Anna Luther,
               Charles Arling,
               Hugh Fay,
               Earl Rodney
DIRECTORS: E.A. Frazee,
               Walter Reed
PICTURED: Fred Mace

silent films. He also salvaged another relic from a '20s movie house — a vintage popcorn machine. And he uses real butter, not "golden topping."

If it weren't for friends collecting old films and sharing them with other devoted movie buffs, I might never have had a chance to see Raymond Griffith's PATHS TO PARADISE or one of "Fatty" Arbuckle's few talkie short subjects, CLOSE RELATIONS (1933). Wonderful vintage films should be preserved and shared, as well as the movie memorabilia associated with them. In some cases, only the paper lobby art has survived; the even more fragile and volatile celluloid has been destroyed. With that in mind, I've talked with friends and fellow collectors about the rare specimens of lobby cards that ought to be included in this volume of classic comedies.

My preference in films has always been the silents, particularly Keaton's and other early comedies. That preference is also reflected in my collection of lobby art, with some of my oldest cards reproduced on these pages. These four lobby cards were part of a batch found at a Florida swap meet ten years ago and,

CHARLES MURRAY with LOUISE FAZENDA in "HER MARBLE HEART" (1916 TRIANGLE distribution)

FORD STERLING with POLLY MORAN in "THE HUNT" (1915 TRIANGLE distribution)

HER MARBLE HEART
1916 Triangle • Keystone
STARRING: Charles Murray,
Louise Fazenda,
Harry Booker,
Frank Hayes
DIRECTOR: F. Richard Jones
PICTURED: Louise Fazenda,
Charles Murray

THE HUNT
1915 Triangle • Keystone
STARRING: Ford Sterling,
Polly Moran,
May Emory,
Bobby Vernon
DIRECTORS: Ford Sterling &
Charley Chase
PICTURED: Bobby Vernon,
May Emory,
Ford Sterling
(in blackface)

because the titles are obscure and most of the players long forgotten, they were not considered to be of much value to most collectors. To me they are priceless. All of the films shown here were produced by the "King of Comedy," actor, director, producer Mack Sennett. When he left Biograph in 1912 to form Keystone, Sennett brought with him Fred Mace, Ford Sterling, and Mabel Normand. Later, his studio roster included Roscoe "Fatty" Arbuckle, Chester Conklin, Al St. John, Edgar Kennedy, Minta Durfee, Mack Swain, Slim Summerville and Charlie Chaplin. With the beginning of the sound era, many of these silent comedy stars were out of work and, by the mid-'30s, already forgotten: Fred Mace (who died in 1917) and Ford Sterling had once been as popular as Chaplin.

Two of the more valuable cards in my collection are those of the Marx Brothers' comedies DUCK SOUP and HORSEFEATHERS. The DUCK SOUP card is one of only two lobbies showing all four of the Marx Brothers. Fifteen years ago, when the card first appeared on the market, another collector beat me to the store and bought the complete set of eight DUCK SOUP cards for the then-exorbitant price of $400. Because of parental pressure ("Why do you want to throw away good money?") the collector sold the set back to the store at a loss. I raced to the shop and paid $50 for the one card I most wanted. That single card is now worth about $2,000; I regret that I couldn't afford to buy the whole set. By contrast, the HORSEFEATHERS card was a gift. I came across a stack of lobby cards that were of no interest to me, but I knew a collector who specialized in that particular genre. He was so grateful for my information that he gave me the Marx Brothers card. It's now worth about $1,000. Keaton is still my favorite performer, and at the top of my shopping list is the lobby card for his first film: THE BUTCHER BOY (1917).

The chief influence on my selections, however, has been the lobby card art. The best designs and most vibrant colors always appear in the earlier cards, with the best examples to be found in the late '20s and early '30s. Even though the films are in black and white, the lobby art was always in color or tinted brown or blue. After World War II, the quality of lobby art deteriorated. While wonderful film comedies continued to be made, most of the lobby card art doesn't warrent inclusion in this collection.

In the end, of course, it's always a question of personal taste. Critics are fond of using food analogies in describing film — "deliciously funny" or "a tasty confection" — and I think it's entirely appropriate. At the 4th of July screening, I joined fellow film buffs to watch early movies that were as carefully chosen as the menu for a banquet — and after our marathon feast, we ate a potluck supper. Why not equate food and film? What could be heartier or more soul-satisfying than a smorgasbord of Keaton, Chaplin and Laurel and Hardy? My mouth waters at the thought of it.

Michael Hawks

Michael Hawks

LOBBY CARDS: THE CLASSIC COMEDIES

THE FIREMAN

1916 · Mutual

Charlie wins the girl in the checkerboard dress (Purviance, his sweetheart in real life, too) after rescuing her from the family home set afire by her father. Two condemned houses were burned to provide the spectacular conflagrations. Arriving at the scene of the blaze, the firemen perform their drill exercises in the style of a music hall chorus before attending to the fire. Much of the film was shot in a real fire station with a stable of engine horses looking on, inspiring Chaplin, during a scene in which he cleans the firehouse, to tidy the horses with a feather duster. In other sequences, plates are dealt like playing cards onto a dinner table and the engine's boilers become a coffee urn as Charlie draws coffee and cream from the taps. During the '30s, actor Lloyd Bacon (Edna's suitor) became one of Warner's most prolific directors.

STARRING: Charles Chaplin, Edna Purviance, Eric Campbell, Albert Austin, Lloyd Bacon, Leo White
PRODUCER: Charles Chaplin
DIRECTOR: Charles Chaplin
WRITTEN BY: Charles Chaplin (Story Collaboration - Vincent Bryan)
PHOTOGRAPHY: Roland Totheroh, William C. Foster
PICTURED: *Lloyd Bacon, Edna Purviance, Charles Chaplin, Eric Campbell*

CHARLIE CHAPLIN
IN
"THE FIREMAN"

© 1916

MUTUAL CHAPLIN

LONE STAR CORPORATION.

ROSCOE ARBUCKLE WITH AL ST. JOHN AND MINTA DURFEE IN HIS WIFE'S MISTAKE—MACK SENNETT PRODUCTION

HIS WIFE'S MISTAKE

1916 · Triangle-Keystone

"Fatty" Arbuckle's movie career began at Selig Studios in 1909 and this two-reeler, filmed in Fort Lee, New Jersey was his 106th film. His wife, Minta (Araminta) Durfee, frequently co-starred with him. The sex-and-drugs-riddled scandal linking Arbuckle to the tragic death of starlet Virginia Rappe in 1921 and the subsequent banning of his films effectively ended his career. He did find some work directing, though primarily only short subjects, and made a brief attempt to revive his performing career by appearing in vaudeville revues. In 1932 he managed to go before the cameras again in a handful of two-reelers that he hoped would be the steppingstone to his former popularity. Before he could re-establish his reputation, he died of a heart attack in New York in 1933.

STARRING: Roscoe Arbuckle, Al St. John, Minta Durfee, Betty Gray
PRODUCER: Mack Sennett
DIRECTOR: Roscoe Arbuckle
PICTURED: *Roscoe Arbuckle, Betty Gray*

A DOG'S LIFE

1918 · First National

In this three-reeler originally entitled I SHOULD WORRY, Chaplin befriends a mongrel dog named Scraps and rescues Edna Purviance from a grim life at a local cabaret. After battling thugs over a stolen wallet, Chaplin emerges victorious and he and his favorite leading lady (and his only one between 1915 and 1923) settle down to the quiet rural life. Exploitation, poverty, hunger and prostitution formed the hard core of Chaplin's view of street-life reality in his first film under contract to First National. Two thousand people signed the visitors' book in January 1918 when Chaplin welcomed the public to see his newly completed studio on Sunset and La Brea. However, Chaplin's good will soured when it was discovered that two guests pretending to be journalists had spent three days eavesdropping outside production meetings. Their sketches and notes pertaining to the production, Chaplin claimed, forced him to scrap $10,000 worth of material he'd devised for the film. It also prompted him to ban the public from all future visits and probably contributed to his secrecy and suspicion in later years. Chaplin had long searched for the ideal "comedy dog" and it's said he housed 21 dogs from the local pound until complaints from the neighbors forced him to reduce the number to a dozen. "Mutt," the charming mongrel who starred in this film, remained on staff at the studio until his death.

STARRING: Charles Chaplin, Edna Purviance, Albert Austin, Henry Bergman, Sydney Chaplin
PRODUCED, WRITTEN AND DIRECTED BY: Charles Chaplin
PHOTOGRAPHY: Roland Totheroh
PRODUCTION DESIGNER: Charles D. Hall
PICTURED: *Charles Chaplin*

BUSTER KEATON

THE BELLBOY

1918 · Paramount-Arbuckle

Begun in early December 1917 and completed within six weeks, this was Arbuckle's 120th film in less than ten years. It was Keaton's ninth film. Arbuckle once commented that Keaton lived in the camera, spending all day devising gags and sequences and the physical or mechanical ways to make them work. Often the two actors went to public screenings together, arriving after the picture started and taking their seats in the dark to avoid recognition. On one occasion, offended by the overheard cynical remark of a moviegoer that actors had doubles to do the dangerous stunts, Arbuckle tapped the woman on the shoulder and said, "Lady, that was no double, that was me!" Keaton's father Joe played a small part in this film as he did in a number of films starring his son in the '20s. Arbuckle tried to keep his rambunctious nephew, Al St. John, out of show business, but the determined youngster finally persuaded his Aunt Minta to pave the way for a meeting with Sennett. A daredevil prankster who loved bicycle tricks, St. John impressed Sennett with every imaginable foolhardy stunt and earned a place in the Keystone company at three dollars a day playing his stock country-rube roles. St. John would gain new found fame in the '40s in a series of popular, though poorly made, films at PRC studios with B-western star Buster Crabbe.

STARRING: Roscoe Arbuckle, Buster Keaton, Al St. John, Alice Lake, Joe Keaton
PRODUCER: Joseph M. Schenck
DIRECTOR, WRITER: Roscoe Arbuckle
PICTURED: *Buster Keaton, Al. St. John, Roscoe Arbuckle, Alice Lake*

THE HAYSEED

1919 · Paramount-Arbuckle

Keaton smiles, a rarity on film, and even rarer to find it reproduced on a lobby card. This was his second short with Arbuckle after Keaton's return from a brief tour of duty with the Army during World War I.

STARRING: Roscoe Arbuckle, Buster Keaton, Molly Malone
PRODUCER: Joseph M. Schenck
DIRECTOR: Roscoe Arbuckle
SCENARIO: Jean Havez
PICTURED: *Roscoe Arbuckle, Molly Malone, Buster Keaton*

ONCE A PLUMBER

1920 · Universal

One of the most popular and polished comedy teams of the World War I era, Lyons and Moran, developed a fast paced, story-oriented humor that was a departure from the slapstick trend of the time. Their snappy, high-class comedies depended upon establishing a familiar situation out of which the gags and spoofs flowed naturally. Slapstick was already on its way out by the time Lyons and Moran became a team in 1915 under the direction of producer Al Christie. Their vaudeville stage training in "keep it moving" kinetic comedy sketches translated easily to the new tastes in film comedy. Their brand of humor became the prototype for an era of motion picture comedy that continued to develop in the Sennett and Roach companies of the '20s. This represents one of the team's last films in their five year union; Moran continued as a character actor in feature films and Lyons went on to produce, direct and star in a series of two-reelers.

STARRING: Eddie Lyons, Lee Moran, George B. Williams, Sidney Dean, Jeff Osborne
DIRECTOR: Eddie Lyons and Lee Moran
STORY: Edgar Franklin
SCENARIO: C.B. Hoadley
PICTURED: *Eddie Lyons, Lee Moran*

THE SUITOR

1920 · Vitagraph

An acrobatic clown who worked in whiteface and most often played a bumbling simpleton, Semon was one of the most popular and highest paid comedians of the '20s. He was the son of professional magician "Zera the Great" and worked as a cartoonist before he joined Vitagraph to write and direct comedy shorts. True to his credo that a comic is secondary to his gags, Semon filmed thinly plotted movies, dependent upon stunt gimmicks and hectic chase sequences. Considered a big spender and a prima donna on set, Semon was further criticized for his endless repetition of cliché gags and for physically appearing only briefly in his starring vehicles. Entire fast paced chase sequences, which constituted the bulk of a Semon comedy, were often filmed with stuntmen Bill Hauber and Richard Talmadge doubling for the diminutive comedian who showed up only to do closeups. Gags were everything to the comic who supposedly carried a priceless notebook in his back pocket; it contained a careful record of his jokes. Semon, who often worked with his wife Dorothy Dwan, fell out with Vitagraph in 1922 and soon faced box office failure with the costly features he produced elsewhere. Once a millionaire, who briefly enjoyed a popularity rivaling that of Chaplin and Lloyd, the broken and bankrupt Semon suffered a nervous breakdown and died of pneumonia in New York in 1928 at the age of thirty-nine.

STARRING: Larry Semon, Lucille Carlisle, Frank Alexander
DIRECTOR: Larry Semon, Norman Taurog
SCENARIO: Larry Semon, Norman Taurog
PICTURED: *Larry Semon*

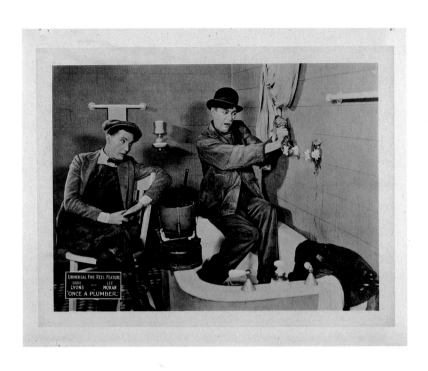

"None of This Foolishness. You Come with Me"

BE MY WIFE

BE MY WIFE

1921 · Goldwyn

Using the pseudonym Max Linder, the great French comedian made films by day for Pathé and by night played in melodramas on the Paris stage under his given name, Gabriel-Maximilien Leuvielle. After three years of this regimen, he decided in 1908 to concentrate on film, and during the years before World War I Max Linder became an internationally famous actor, writer and director. During his service as a soldier, he suffered gas poisoning, which severely damaged his physical and mental health. He tried to make a comeback in French films, and then made his American debut with the Essanay company in 1917. After only three films, the urbane, dapper comedian suffered an attack of pneumonia that left him incapacitated for a year. In 1919 he formed his own production company to make three more films, including BE MY WIFE, but poor box office reception and his continued ill health left him broken and embittered. He returned to France, married the daughter of a restaurateur and two years later, after a poor showing in two European films, he entered a suicide pact with his wife. On October 30, 1925 he and his wife were found dead in a Paris hotel room. His final American film was the brilliant parody of Fairbanks' THE THREE MUSKETEERS; THE THREE MUST-GET-THERES. Upon learning of his esteemed colleague's death, Chaplin paid homage to the screen's first real comedian by closing his studios for the day.

STARRING: Max Linder, Alta Allen, Caroline Rankin, Lincoln Stedman, Rose Dione
PRODUCER, DIRECTOR, WRITER: Max Linder
PHOTOGRAPHY: Charles J. Van Enger
PICTURED: *Alta Allen, Max Linder, Caroline Rankin*

THE KID

1921 · First National

Chaplin's first feature film was a critical and financial success, a gratifying vindication for the gifted artist who defied the prevailing wisdom against mixing slapstick with drama. Chaplin "adopts" the abandoned baby of an unwed mother (Purviance) and trains the streetwise urchin (Coogan) to hurl rocks at windows so the Tramp can arrive on the scene as an itinerant glazier. When welfare authorities attempt to remove the boy from his custody, the Tramp hides the Kid in a rooming house. Its owner tries to abduct the child for a reward. The distraught Tramp is awakened from a dream by a policeman who reunites him with the Kid and his mother, now a wealthy and renowned opera singer. Partially autobiographical, with scenes drawn from Chaplin's own grim childhood memories, this poignant film presents realistic characters in a well constructed plot. Its innovative blend of comedy and pathos marked a significant turning point in Chaplin's career and launched five-year-old Coogan as the most beloved child actor of the '20s. Chaplin discovered the boy in a vaudeville act, hoofing in imitation of his father Jack — who appears in the film as a bum, the devil and a party guest. Chaplin had to comfort and reassure the boy during production when the elder Coogan bullied his son into crying on cue by threatening to send him to a work house. Only three weeks before shooting began, Chaplin's three-day-old son died, prompting many to believe that this tragedy accounted for his particular affection for Coogan. After 18 months in production, at a cost to Chaplin of $500,000, First National was willing to pay only about $400,000 for the film. It was also apparent that the studio was in collusion with Chaplin's estranged wife Mildred to attach his assets during their nasty divorce proceedings. To safeguard his film, Chaplin conspired with cinematographer Totheroh and others to hide the 400,000 feet of negative in coffee tins and convey it by train to Salt Lake City where the highly inflammable nitrate film was edited. Chaplin successfully negotiated with Mildred and the studio lawyers, enabling him to open the film in New York on June 1, 1921 — to instant and phenomenal success. Within three years the feature was distributed to 50 countries throughout the world. Ironically, one of the players in the dream sequence was twelve-year-old Lillita McMurray, later Lita Gray, who became Chaplin's wife four years later. In time she presented Chaplin with a similarly messy divorce scenario during the production of THE CIRCUS (1928).

STARRING: Charles Chaplin, Jackie Coogan, Edna Purviance, Carl Miller
PRODUCER, DIRECTOR, WRITER: Charles Chaplin
ASSOCIATE DIRECTOR: Charles Reisner
PHOTOGRAPHER: Roland Totheroh
PICTURED: *Tom Wilson, Charles Chaplin, Jackie Coogan*

Charles Chaplin

IN

THE KID

written and directed
by Charles Chaplin

6 REELS OF JOY

A FIRST NATIONAL
ATTRACTION

"The cop's after the Kid for raising a riot of laughter!"

JOSEPH M. SCHENCK
PRESENTS
BUSTER KEATON
IN
HARD LUCK

METRO PICTURES

HARD LUCK

1921 · Metro

Alone, hungry and hounded by the police, Keaton again appears as the man the world has turned against. In this silent short, Keaton attempts suicide by a variety of methods, each successive effort a perfectly motivated study in finely honed slapstick craftsmanship. Ironically, it's after he finally gives up the idea of killing himself that his life is threatened when he joins a country club and thwarts an attack by a gang of thieves. To prove to the audience that what they saw was not an editing trick, Keaton often performed his stunts in a long shot without a cut. In HARD LUCK Keaton plunged from a fifty-foot platform to a swimming pool, missed it and crashed through marble paving (paper covered with wax). While risking life and limb for the sake of his craft, Keaton broke his leg in 1922 and his neck in 1924. Virginia Fox, his leading lady in this and several other Keaton shorts, later became the wife of studio mogul Darryl F. Zanuck. In France, where Keaton's popularity was enormous, this film was known as LA GUIGNE DE MALEC.

STARRING: Buster Keaton, Virginia Fox, Joe Roberts
PRODUCER: Joseph M. Schenck
WRITER AND DIRECTOR: Buster Keaton and Eddie Cline
PICTURED: *Buster Keaton*

THE IDLE CLASS

1921 · First National

Chaplin portrays both a tramp and a gentleman of wealth in this two-reeler about an unhappy marriage — an irony because Chaplin's own marriage was suffering during the five months of filming. Chaplin's future wife Lita Grey and her mother have roles as Edna Purviance's maids. Seeking inspiration, Chaplin rummaged through the studio's cluttered prop room and uncovered some old golf clubs — and thus came the idea to explore high society and to play the dual roles of a drunken socialite and the Tramp. In a stunning reversal of pathos to slapstick, the Socialite pathetically turns away from a photograph of his wife who has threatened to leave him because of his drinking. Seen from behind, the convulsive movement of his shoulders leads one to think he's weeping in sorrow for his failed marriage, but the true cause of his agitation is revealed when he turns back to pour a well-shaken martini. This was one of five pictures completed to fulfill his First National contract requirements before he could embark on the United Artists co-venture with Pickford, Fairbanks and Griffith.

STARRING: Charles Chaplin, Edna Purviance, Henry Bergman, Mack Swain
PRODUCER, WRITER, DIRECTOR: Charles Chaplin
PHOTOGRAPHER: Roland Totheroh
SECOND CAMERA: Jack Wilson
ASSISTANT: Charles Reisner
PRODUCTION DESIGNER: Charles D. Hall
PICTURED: *Charles Chaplin*

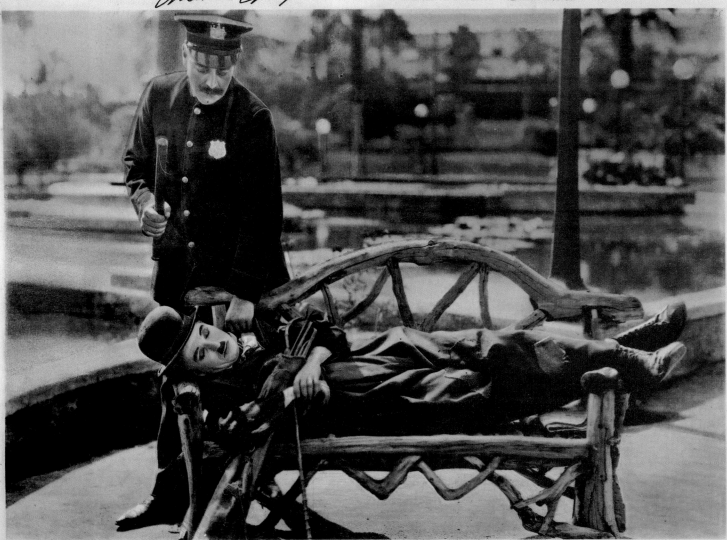

Charles Chaplin IN 'THE IDLE CLASS"

A man of leisure.

JOSEPH M. SCHENCK
presents
BUSTER KEATON
in
OUR HOSPITALITY
Story and titles by
JEAN HAVEZ
JOE MITCHELL
CLYDE BRUCKMAN
A METRO PICTURE
IN 7 PARTS
Directed by
BUSTER KEATON
JACK BLYSTONE

BUSTER KEATON in OUR HOSPITALITY
A METRO PICTURE (IN 7 PARTS)

BUSTER KEATON in OUR HOSPITALITY
A METRO PICTURE (IN 7 PARTS)

BUSTER KEATON in OUR HOSPITALITY
A METRO PICTURE (IN 7 PARTS)

OUR HOSPITALITY

1923 · Metro

Based on the age-old Hatfield and McCoy feud (with the names changed to Canfield and McKay) this wonderful film is filled with Keaton's touch for authenticity and contains one of his most breathtaking stunts. Renowned for rarely using a double, Keaton was nearly drowned in the rapids performing this dangerous stunt that had him swept down a river toward a waterfall. In the story he is temporarily saved from going over when a piece of rope tied around his waist snags itself on a log. Momentarily safe, he sees his girl also imperiled and in the nick of time he swings out, grasps her and pulls her to safety on a nearby ledge. A lightweight dummy doubled for film girlfriend Talmadge, who was his real-life wife and a sister of '20s screen stars Constance and Norma. Location filming was in the High Sierras near Lake Tahoe. Keaton, during this happy period of his life, made it a family affair. Three generations of the Keaton family are represented: father Joseph, and fifteen-month-old son Joe, and Keaton's pregnant wife who, toward the end of filming, couldn't appear in profile. In a clever stunt Keaton has a locomotive hurtle full-throttle toward a tunnel that appears to be too small. When disaster seems imminent, it's revealed that the tunnel is shaped like a bottle with the train's smokestack accomodated by the part corresponding to the neck of the bottle. A great success, this production cost $208,000 and grossed over $1,500,00. A replica of a Gentleman's Hobbyhorse — an early form of bicycle — was produced as a prop for this film and the Smithsonian, unable to locate an authentic example, acquired the copy for their display. Unique among his films and reflecting Keaton's own happiness while making it, this story is told without a trace of bitterness.

STARRING: Buster Keaton, Natalie Talmadge, Joe Roberts, Joseph Keaton Sr.
PRODUCER: Joseph M. Schenck
DIRECTOR: Buster Keaton, John Blystone
STORY, SCENARIO, TITLES: Jean Havez, Joseph Mitchell, Clyde Bruckman
PICTURED: *Buster Keaton*

THE SHRIEK OF ARABY

1923 · Allied Producers and Distributors

After Valentino's enormous success with THE SHEIK (1921), Turpin trod the desert sands in similar adventures as the cross-eyed hero left in charge of the throne when an Arabian prince goes on vacation. Known as one of Hollywood's richest yet stingiest men, he began working in movies in 1907. After a shaky start appearing in shorts for the Essanay company, Turpin returned to burlesque where he created the character "Happy Hooligan". In 1914 he bounded back into films playing Chaplin's foil in a series of comedies. It was an uneasy relationship that Chaplin abruptly ended when it appeared Turpin was beginning to rival him in popularity. Turpin found his greatest success in parody, utilizing his unique and ludicrous appearance to burlesque Latin lover Valentino and Teutonic heavy Von Stroheim. Realizing that his face was his fortune, the canny comedian insured his eyes with Lloyds of London against uncrossing. No longer a star after the talkies arrived, Turpin's wise investments enabled him to retire gracefully, though he continued to do cameo roles until his death in 1940 at the age of 76.

STARRING: Ben Turpin, Kathryn McGuire, George Cooper, Charles Stevenson
PRODUCER: Mack Sennett
DIRECTOR: F. Richard Jones
STORY: Mack Sennett
PICTURED: *Kathryn McGuire, Ben Turpin*

MACK SENNETT
PRESENTS
"THE SHRIEK OF ARABY"

MACK SENNETT

presents

MABEL
NORMAND

in

"The
Extra Girl"

DIRECTED BY
F. RICHARD JONES

ASSOCIATED EXHIBITORS
ARTHUR S. KANE, President

PHYSICAL DISTRIBUTORS
PATHE EXCHANGE, INC.

COUNTRY OF ORIGIN U.S.A.

SUE GRAHAM HAD NO DESIRE TO SUPPLY
ANY JUNGLE MONARCH WITH A MEAL TICKET.

WYANDAK, N.Y.C.

THE EXTRA GIRL

1923 · Associated Exhibitors

This endearing comedy about a small town girl who wins a movie contest and goes to Hollywood to seek her fortune provides a fascinating behind-the-scenes view of '20s film-making. While appearing on-screen as the irrepressible Sue Graham who runs into problems with a studio lion, Normand's personal life was an entanglement of drugs, scandal and ill health. In 1922 she was implicated in the still-unsolved murder of director William Desmond Taylor with whom she was thought to be romantically involved. Her reputation was further tarnished on New Year's Eve 1923 when her chauffeur wounded a wealthy friend of hers in a late-night scuffle. Although she declared her innocence in both cases and was never indicted for either crime, the guilt by association notoriety and her well-publicized party-girl antics effectively destroyed her career. Hounded in the headlines and beset by deteriorating health, Normand left Hollywood in 1925 to launch herself on Broadway in THE LITTLE MOUSE. THE EXTRA GIRL was her last feature, and she ended her film career with a series of five shorts for producer Hal Roach in 1926-1927. Her efforts met with failure and the woman Chaplin described as "lighthearted and gay, a good fellow... kind and generous", died of Tuberculosis in 1930 at the age of 38.

STARRING: Mabel Normand, Ralph Graves, George Nichols, Anna Hernandez, Vernon Dent
PRODUCER: Mack Sennett
DIRECTOR: F. Richard Jones
SCENARIO: Bernard McConville
STORY: Mack Sennett
PICTURED: *Mabel Normand*

WHY WORRY

1923 · Pathé

Wealthy hypochondriac Harold Van Pelham (Lloyd) visits a South American country in the midst of a revolution and, with the aid of a giant (Aasen), he quells the revolt. In so doing, he rids himself of his imaginary illnesses and marries his nurse (Ralston). Designating his fictional country in turmoil as "The Isle of Paradiso, A Mythical Island Somewhere, In Some Body of Water" was Lloyd's sensitive and soothing response to Mexicans who believed their homeland was being lampooned. In October 1923 Lloyd addressed an apologetic letter to the Mexican Consul-General and made sure that all prints and advertising material deleted any reference to his country. Prior to shooting, there was a major problem when eight-foot-plus circus giant George Auger dropped dead the day before he was to leave the East coast for filming in California. The search for a replacement finally led to 503-pound John Aasen of Minneapolis who measured 8' 9 1/2" tall. Ralston, who later married film star Richard Arlen, debuted as Lloyd's leading lady in this comedy, her first of six features with him.

STARRING: Harold Lloyd, Jobyna Ralston, John Aasen, Leo White, James Mason
PRODUCER: Hal Roach
DIRECTOR: Fred Newmeyer, Sam Taylor
STORY: Sam Taylor, Ted Wilde, Tim Whelan
PHOTOGRAPHY: Walter Lundin
PICTURED: *John Aasen, Harold Lloyd*

HAL ROACH
PRESENTS

HAROLD LLOYD

IN

"Why Worry?"

HIS LATEST SIX REEL

Pathécomedy

TRADE 🐓 MARK

Two to a Door; One to Adore

Country of origin and
production, U.S.A.

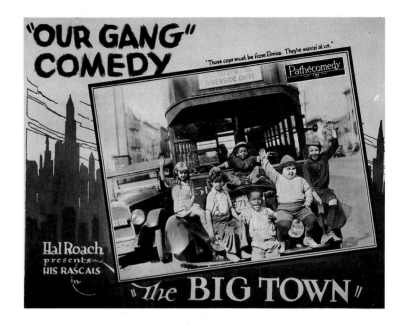

OUR GANG COMEDIES

DOGS OF WAR

1923 · Pathé

The great battlefield is a tomato patch with the Our Gang troops hurling overripe vegetables until the pretty Red Cross nurse (Kornman) is pulled from combat to do some acting at a nearby movie studio. The behind-the-scenes look at the Roach Studios and a cameo appearance by Harold Lloyd are added attractions to this fast-paced, funny two-reeler.

STARRING: Mickey Daniels, Mary Kornman, Jack Davis, Ernie Morrison, Jackie Condon, Joe Cobb, Allen "Farina" Hoskins, Monty O'Grady and Andy Samuels
PRODUCER: Hal Roach
DIRECTOR: Robert F. McGowan
STORY: Hal E. Roach
PICTURED: *Mickey Daniels, Jackie Condon, Ernie Morrison. (In cameo) Mary Kornman, "Farina"*

BETTER MOVIES

1925 · Pathé

The Our Gang team produce a neighborhood movie.

STARRING: Jackie Condon, Mickey Daniels, Billy Lord, Jay R. Smith, Mary Kornman, Johnny Downs, Joe Cobb, Allen "Farina" Hoskins, Jackie Hanes, Bobby Young, Lyle Tayo
PRODUCER: Hal Roach
DIRECTOR: Robert F. McGowan
STORY: Hal Roach
TITLES: H. M. Walker
PICTURED: *Jay R. Smith, Jackie Condon, Johnny Downs, Mary Kornman, Mickey Daniels, Joe Cobb, Martha Sleeper, "Farina"*

THE BIG TOWN

1925 · Pathé

Accidentally trapped while playing in an empty boxcar, Our Gang find themselves on an overnight journey to New York City. Their adventures are curtailed once New York's finest round them up and send them back home to their angry mothers and spankings all around.

STARRING: Mickey Daniels, Mary Kornman, Jackie Condon, Joe Cobb, Allen "Farina" Hoskins, Eugene Jackson
PRODUCER: Hal Roach
DIRECTOR: Robert F. McGowan
TITLES: H. M. Walker
PICTURED: *Mary Kornman, Jackie Condon, Eugene Jackson, Allen "Farina" Hoskins, Joe Cobb, Mickey Daniels*

BABY CLOTHES

1926 · Pathé

A swindling couple must produce two children for whom a rich uncle has been sending support money. Our Gang members Joe and Mickey are pressed into service, wearing curly wigs and baby clothes. The plot becomes hectic and confusing when a practical-joke-playing midget, and then Farina, also try to pass themselves off as the couple's children.

STARRING: Joe Cobb, Mickey Daniels, Mary Kornman, Johnny Downs, Allen "Farina" Hoskins, Jackie Condon, Bobby Young
PRODUCER: Hal Roach
DIRECTOR: Robert F. McGowan
STORY: Hal E. Roach
PICTURED: *Mickey Daniels, "Farina," Jackie Condon, Joe Cobb, William Gillespie*

SHERLOCK, JR.

1924 · Metro

In what is unquestionably one of Keaton's most inventive films, his escapades include diving head first into a suitcase and disappearing; leaping through an open window from inside a house and reappearing on the outside fully clothed in a woman's dress; and the brilliant sequence in which, as a motion picture projectionist, he falls asleep on the job and then literally walks into the film showing on screen. Keaton, who has dreamed himself into the action of the film, has difficulty adjusting to the plot of the picture. The locations shift in a series of cuts, and a hapless Keaton is projected from a walk down a street to the treacherous ledge of a cliff to an exotic jungle scene. In a virtuoso performance much appreciated by audiences, well aware that Keaton did not use doubles in his dangerous stunts, he crossed a forty-foot gap in a broken aquaduct across the roofs of two moving vans at the exact moment that they meet and pass. After the 1921 scandal that destroyed Roscoe "Fatty" Arbuckle's career, Doris Dean, his second wife, claimed that he often did uncredited work with his friend Keaton — including writing and directing this classic.

STARRING: Buster Keaton, Kathryn McGuire, Ward Crane, Joseph Keaton
PRODUCER: Joseph M. Schenck
DIRECTOR: Buster Keaton
STORY: Clyde Bruckman, Jean Havez, Joseph Mitchell
PICTURED: *Buster Keaton*

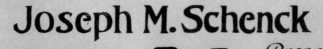

Joseph M. Schenck

Presents

Buster Keaton

in

Sherlock, Jr.

Directed by BUSTER KEATON

Story by
Jean Havez, Joseph Mitchell,
Clyde Bruckman.

METRO PICTURE

A Pathé Picture

The Dog's Out of the Bag!

HAROLD LLOYD
IN "GIRL SHY"

GIRL SHY

1924 · Pathé

True to his screen persona, Lloyd is again magically transformed from a shy dunderhead to a dynamic man of action when the girl of his dreams is in jeopardy. In his wild race against time to rescue Ralston from a mock marriage, Lloyd is sidetracked at every turn as he incorporates all possible means of transporting himself to the church. He misses his train, hitches a ride in a car that promptly swings into a driveway, steals a car loaded with whisky and is chased by the cops and the bootleggers. He commandeers a truck that can't negotiate a narrow mountain road and — after encounters with dead cats, frightened horses and a stray fire truck — seizes control of a trolley and whizzes through the city streets at full speed. In an inspired sequence of comedic events, daredevil Lloyd climbs to the top of the trolley to reconnect the power and is left dangling as the trolley surges down the track at fullthrottle. Lloyd drops into the back of an automobile, abandons it for a passing motorcycle, and finally arrives at the church riding a horse bareback. The Our Gang kids, Joe Cobb and Mickey Daniels made unbilled appearances early in the film to reciprocate Lloyd's comic turn in their 1923 film DOGS OF WAR.

STARRING: Harold Lloyd, Jobyna Ralston, Richard Daniels, Carlton Griffin, Joe Cobb, Mickey Daniels
PRODUCER: Hal Roach
DIRECTOR: Fred Newmeyer, Sam Taylor
STORY: Sam Taylor, Ted Wilde, Tim Whelan, Tommy Gray
PHOTOGRAPHY: Walter Lundin and Henry N. Kohler
PICTURED: *Jobyna Ralston, Harold Lloyd*

CHARLEY'S AUNT

1925 · Producers Distributing Corporation

Chaplin's half-brother Syd triumphed as a female impersonator in this movie adaptation of the Brandon Thomas stage play, and his success kept him in skirts through two more films. The brothers, who had shared a bleak childhood of hunger and orphanage life, both turned to the stage where slapstick, pantomime and rollicking song and dance were the staples of English music hall. Masquerading as a woman for comic effect was always a crowd pleaser and Syd reveled in vulgar, low-brow clowning. Four years Charlie's senior, he hit the big time with Fred Karno's famous troupe, then introduced his brother to the company. Some years later, Charlie returned the favor by bringing Syd into Sennett's Keystone films in Hollywood. Early contemporaries reckoned that Syd's comic skills were superior to Charlie's. Despite ample evidence of Syd's pantomime talents in A DOG'S LIFE, he stuck to knockabout slapstick and never developed the distinctive style of his brother. Syd eventually left Keystone because of his strained relationship with Sennett, who found much of his humor too suggestively vulgar and censored the more offensive material. However, both Chaplins profited handsomely from Syd's business acumen (for instance, he originated the procedure — now standard — of renting films on a percentage based on theatre capacity). Syd, who never acquired American citizenship, returned to England because of problems with the Internal Revenue Service. Sustaining close and affectionate bonds with his brother, Syd continued to manage all of Charlie's business affairs.

STARRING: Syd Chaplin, Ethel Shannon, Lucien Littlefield, Alec B. Francis
PRODUCER: Al and Charles Christie
DIRECTOR: Scott Sidney
SCENARIO: F. McGrew Willis
PICTURED: *Ethel Shannon, Jimmy Harrison, Eulalie Jensen, Lucien Littlefield, Syd Chaplin, Philips Smalley, David James*

The funniest farce in forty years

"Charley's Aunt" with Syd Chaplin

Produced by CHRISTIE

RELEASED BY
Producers Distributing
CORPORATION

"Enough to make a cat laugh!"

HAROLD LLOYD

in

"The FRESHMAN"

Is'nt it wonderful to be in love?

A Pathé Picture

Produced by HAROLD LLOYD CORPORATION

THE FRESHMAN

1925 · Pathé

In this quintessential '20s college picture, Harold Lamb (Lloyd) triumphs over his campus misadventures to win the girl of his dreams (Ralston). At a time when attending college was for the chosen few, the fun and frolic, romance and glamour of campus life was the subject of intense and envious public interest. This popular satire was a collaborative effort that Lloyd credited to his entire writing staff. Ironically, the script became the subject of a lawsuit that was not settled until 1933. Lloyd and business manager William Fraser had discussed their scenario for THE FRESHMAN during a luncheon with pulp writer H. C. Witmer, who described his own football story, "The Emancipation of Rodney". Although his tale was unsuitable for Lloyd's use, Witmer sued; his estate won a favorable verdict in 1930 which was reversed three years later. Lloyd discovered that shooting the ending first didn't work for this venture, as it had for SAFETY LAST, and scrapped the football scenes he'd filmed at the beginning of his schedule at the Pasadena Rose Bowl. Later, Lloyd dropped a painful scene that preview audiences hated in which fellow students at a soda shop divest Lloyd of nearly all his money while flattering him to his face and jeering behind his back. In another scene, when Lloyd knocks down the campus rake who's been forcing his attentions on Ralston, the cad retaliates by claiming that the entire campus considers Lloyd a joke. Devastated by the scorn and unable to maintain a manly display of indifference, Lloyd collapses in the lap of his sweetheart and weeps. Lloyd removed this scene because he felt it was emotionally excessive.

STARRING: Harold Lloyd, Jobyna Ralston, Brooks Benedict
PRODUCER: Hal Roach
DIRECTOR: Sam Taylor, Fred Newmeyer
SCENARIO: Sam Taylor, John Grey, Ted Wilde, Tim Whelan, Clyde Bruckman, Lex Neal, Jean Havez, Brooks B. Harding
PHOTOGRAPHY: Walter Lundin and Henry N. Kohler
PICTURED: *Harold Lloyd, Jobyna Ralston*

TRAMP, TRAMP, TRAMP

1926 · First National

In his first feature-length film, Langdon is the penniless son who enters a cross-country walking race to win money to pay for his father's operation. Joan Crawford (on loan from MGM and only a step from stardom) plays the daughter of the millionaire shoe manufacturer sponsoring the race. The rich man's advertising ploy is to line the route of the race with enormous billboards featuring his daughter who will present the winner's prize. The scene in which an overwhelmed and awkwardly shy Langdon first meets the heiress and recognizes her famous face from the posters required numerous takes: newcomer Crawford could not keep a straight face. The film was well received by both the press and the public, but popular and talented Langdon nevertheless suffered by the critical comparison to Chaplin. One of the finest comedians of the silent era, Langdon had a rags-to-riches-to-rags career, marked by a meteoric rise from two-reelers beginning in 1924 to starring roles in features for three years, followed by a swift decline to vaudeville, film shorts, and bankruptcy by 1931. The son of Salvation Army officers, Langdon joined a midwestern medicine show in his youth and spent 20 years touring with minstrel shows, circuses and vaudeville before joining Mack Sennett in 1923. The baby-faced clown, wearing the pantomimist's traditional white makeup, created an infantile wide-eyed simpleton who dressed in a tightly buttoned, childlike fashion. The key ingredient to his leap to stardom was the combined creative talents of director Harry Edwards and screenwriter Frank Capra. But, cocky with success, Langdon dropped the pair and began writing and directing his own vehicles. The results were disastrous and First National dropped his contract. As naive and inept in his personal life as the character he portrayed on screen, Langdon was simply not capable of mustering the business skills or creative initiative to make a comeback. The sound era arrived and Langdon's comedy style was sadly outdated.

STARRING: Harry Langdon, Joan Crawford, Edwards Davis, Alec B. Francis
DIRECTOR: Harry Edwards
STORY: Frank Capra, Tim Whelan, Hal Conklin, J. Frank Holliday, Gerald Duffy, Murray Roth
PICTURED: *Harry Langdon*

The Ullman Mfg. Co., N. Y.

Made in U.S.A.

HARRY LANGDON

HARRY
LANGDON
Corporation
presents

in

"Tramp,
tramp,
tramp"

Story by Frank Capra, Tim Whelan,
Hal Conklin, J. Frank Holliday,
Gerald Duffy and Murray Roth —
Directed by HARRY EDWARDS

6 REELS OF
LONG
LANGDON
LAUGHS

A First National Picture

The world's
greatest comedian

RAYMOND GRIFFITH

"HANDS UP"

WITH MARION NIXON

A Paramount Picture

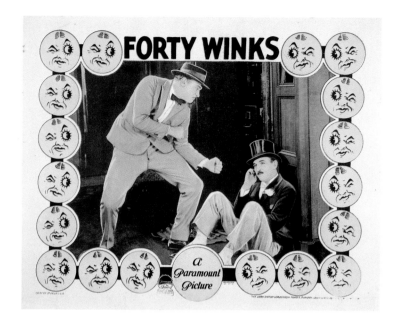

FORTY WINKS

A Paramount Picture

RAYMOND GRIFFITH

IN "HE'S A PRINCE!"

WITH MARY BRIAN

A Paramount Picture

RAYMOND GRIFFITH

IN "WET PAINT"

A Paramount Picture

RAYMOND GRIFFITH

HANDS UP

1926 · Paramount

In his escapades as a Civil War spy, Griffith displays his trademark imperturbability by juggling the affections of two sisters he loves and distracting a firing squad by hurling dinner plates that become an alternative target to himself. A deft and inventive pantomimist, Griffith specialized in characters who never lose their cool even though (as in this case) bombarded by artillery and attacked by Indians. In the silent-comedy pantheon, Walter Kerr listed Griffith fifth — after Chaplin, Keaton, Lloyd and Langdon — but only a few of his films remain to confirm his great comedic skills. Most of his films have been lost, but the scattering of prints that remain reveal a unique and fascinating screen presence. His starring career came to an abrupt halt with the beginning of sound because an injury to his vocal cords destroyed his speaking voice and left him with a hoarse whisper. His final role was that of the dying Belgian soldier in ALL QUIET ON THE WESTERN FRONT (1930). As a producer with 20th Century-Fox, Griffith was associated with late '30s films such as HEIDI and DRUMS ALONG THE MOHAWK.

STARRING: Raymond Griffith, Marion Nixon, Virginia Lee Corbin, Mack Swain
DIRECTOR: Clarence Badger
SCENARIO: Monty Brice, Lloyd Corrigan
STORY: Reginald Morris
PICTURED: *Marion Nixon, Raymond Griffith, Virginia Lee Corbin*

FORTY WINKS

1925 · Paramount

STARRING: Viola Dana, Raymond Griffith, Theodore Roberts, Cyril Chadwick, Anna Mae Wong, William Boyd
DIRECTOR: Frank Urson, Paul Iribe
SCREENPLAY: Bertram Millhauser
PHOTOGRAPHY: Peverell Marley
PICTURED: *Raymond Griffith*

HE'S A PRINCE

1925 · Paramount

STARRING: Raymond Griffith, Mary Brian, Tyrone Power Sr., Edgar Norton
DIRECTOR: Edward Sutherland
SCREENPLAY: Keene Thompson
STORY: Reginald Morris, Joseph Mitchell
PHOTOGRAPHY: Charles Boyle
(Although copyrighted with the above title, the film was released as A REGULAR FELLOW.)
PICTURED: *Mary Brian, Raymond Griffith*

WET PAINT

1926 · Paramount

STARRING: Raymond Griffith, Helene Costello, Bryant Washburn, Natalie Kingston, Henry Kolker
DIRECTOR: Arthur Rosson
SCREENPLAY: Lloyd Corrigan
STORY: Reginald Morris
PHOTOGRAPHY: William Marshall
PICTURED: *Natalie Kingston, Raymond Griffith, Henry Kolker*

CHARLIE CHASE

MAMA BEHAVE

1926 · Pathé

"Funny enough to make a blind man laugh," claimed a trade review in *Motion Picture World* when this popular silent was released. Chase, who was devoted to comedy and had a reputation for being as funny offscreen as on, was perhaps the most popular and important star at Roach through the '20s. Most often appearing as the bashful, dapper man about town or the amiable, henpecked husband, the slim, good-looking Chase embodied all the failures, frustrations and humiliations of the common man. He made only five features and excelled in short subjects in a multifaceted career as actor, writer and director, which began at Christie studios in 1913. Brother of director James Parrott, he began using his real name, Charles Parrott, when he joined the Hal Roach studios in 1921 and found his greatest success as a director-writer. In 1924 he switched back to acting under his pseudonym and, when talkies came in, his pleasant singing voice added to his charming screen presence. He joined Columbia Studios in 1937 where he starred in a new series of shorts and directed a number of Three Stooges and Andy Clyde comedies. His role as the obnoxious practical joker at a Shriner's convention is memorable in the Laurel and Hardy feature SONS OF THE DESERT (1934). He died of a heart attack in 1940 at the age of 46. Leading lady Mildred Harris was Charlie Chaplin's wife between 1918 and 1920. Director Leo McCarey, who claimed to owe his successful career to what he learned in his early work with Chase, went on to direct the best of the Laurel and Hardy films, the Marx Brothers classic DUCK SOUP and win Oscars for THE AWFUL TRUTH and GOING MY WAY.

STARRING: Charley Chase, Mildred Harris, Vivian Oakland, Syd Crosley
PRODUCER: Hal Roach
DIRECTOR: Leo McCarey
PICTURED: *Mildred Harris, Charley Chase, Paul Howard's Quality Serenaders*

BE YOUR AGE

1926 · Pathé

STARRING: Charley Chase, Gladys Hulette, Lillian Leighton, Oliver Hardy, Frank Brownlee
SUPERVISOR: F. Richard Jones
DIRECTOR: Leo McCarey
TITLES: H. M. Walker
PICTURED: Lillian Leighton, Charley Chase

HIS WOODEN WEDDING

1925 · Pathé

STARRING: Charley Chase, Katherine Grant, Gale Henry, Fred DeSilva, John Cossar
SUPERVISOR: F. Richard Jones
DIRECTOR: Leo McCarey
TITLES: H. M. Walker
PICTURED: *Charley Chase*

HAROLD LLOYD

IN 'THE KID BROTHER'

PRODUCED BY HAROLD LLOYD CORPORATION   A PARAMOUNT RELEASE

THE KID BROTHER

1927 · Paramount

Playing Harold Hickory, the weakling son of a strong-willed country sheriff, Lloyd finally gets to show his mettle by subduing the villain (Romanoff), both of whom are seen here in a chase sequence aboard a wrecked ship. Relegated to domestic chores in this he-man household, Lloyd displays a clever resourcefulness by tying the laundry to a rope, washing the clothes in a butter churn and then attaching the clothesline to a balloon which sails them aloft to dry. A charming innovation occurs in the scene when Lloyd, who can't bear his sweetheart's (Jobyna's) departure, climbs a tree to watch her dwindle to a tiny figure. He shouts "Goodbye" and her faint response appears on the titles in tiny, four-point type. Also appearing in this film is Jocko the monkey who was featured the following year in Keaton's film, THE CAMERAMAN. With THE MOUNTAIN BOY as its working title, THE KID BROTHER was in production for eight months and was shot on location in the rugged California terrain around Santa Ana, Catalina Island and Placentia. Regarded by many as Lloyd's finest film — because of the fine production values and seamless flow of comic action — it was nevertheless a boxoffice disappointment.

STARRING: Harold Lloyd, Jobyna Ralston, Walter James, Leo Willis, Constantine Romanoff
PRODUCER: Harold Lloyd
DIRECTOR: Ted Wilde, J. A. Howe
STORY: John Grey, Tom Crizer, Ted Wilde
SCENARIO: John Grey, Lex Neal, Howard Green
PHOTOGRAPHY: Walter Lundin and Henry N. Kohler
PICTURED: *Harold Lloyd, Constantine Romanoff*

LONG PANTS

1927 · First National

In the last of Langdon's trio of successful features, he plays a country rube at odds with city slickers and simmering in a romantic stew with a home-town girl (Bennett) and a gangster's moll (Brockwell). Throughout the shooting, director Frank Capra was at wit's end with the puffed-up and difficult star who, swayed by misguided advisors and ego-flattering reviews, demanded to play more pathos in his comedy — "like Chaplin." He fired Capra before the film was completed because, in further emulation of Chaplin, he believed he could also write and direct his starring vehicles. He was a dismal failure in his film-making attempts and, with his uncooperative attitude, was never able to regain his earlier claim to stardom. Capra said of him: "He was the most tragic figure I ever came across in show business."

STARRING: Harry Langdon, Gladys Brockwell, Alan Roscoe, Alma Bennett
DIRECTOR: Frank Capra
STORY: Arthur Ripley
ADAPTATION: Robert Eddy
PICTURED: *Harry Langdon, Alma Bennett*

The Ullman Mfg. Co., N. Y.
Made in U.S.A.
Harry Langdon
IN
LONG
PANTS
Their romance blossomed by the way side.
FIRST NATIONAL PICTURES
A First National Picture

STEAMBOAT BILL, JR.

1928 · United Artists

Home from college and facing his rough-hewn father's (Torrence's) disappointment in him, Keaton has the opportunity to affirm his own rugged manhood by rescuing his steamboat-captain father and new-found sweetheart (Byron) from a savage cyclone. Keaton, never one to use a stunt-double himself, had to substitute his sister Louise for nonswimmer Byron in the cyclone sequence. In one memorable scene during the storm, a house collapses around Keaton while he is standing outside, but his life is spared because he is positioned like a peg to pass through the slot created by an open window. (Keaton later claimed that director Charles Reisner stayed in his tent reading *Science and Health* while the gag was being filmed.) Indeed, Keaton had figured it closely with the clearance of the window exactly three inches over his head and to the side of each shoulder. The facade of the house weighed two tons, its bulk and weight necessary to withstand the strong winds. The picture was filmed in northern California, the Sacramento River doubling for the Mississippi. Initially, Keaton had intended to use a disastrous flood for his story but, because of the widespread damage caused by the real Mississippi floods at the time, it was decided to spare the victims the sight of a devastating reminder on film. Sets had to be rebuilt, stunts re-rigged and costly props shipped to the location to accomodate the new scenario. The considerable delay robbed Keaton of a fall release and the additional expense contributed to the poor boxoffice returns. Following this film, Keaton gave up his own studio and signed with MGM in a move he later considered to be the worst mistake of his career because it meant relinquishing artistic control of his work.

STARRING: Buster Keaton, Ernest Torrence, Marion Byron, Tom Lewis
PRODUCER: Joseph M. Schenck
DIRECTOR: Charles Reisner
STORY, SCENARIO, TITLES: Carl Harbaugh
PICTURED: *Marion Byron, Buster Keaton*

THE CIRCUS

1928 · United Artists

The Little Tramp happens upon an impoverished traveling circus and is chased into the ring by the police, where his antics prove to be an unexpected crowd pleaser. He joins the circus and falls in love with the show's leading lady (Kennedy) whom he must protect from her brutal father. In the end she rejects him for his handsome rival, Rex the High Wire Walker (Crocker), whom Chaplin tries to emulate in a daredevil tightrope act — during which monkeys attack him, rip off his trousers and reveal, to his dismay, that he's forgotten to put on his tights. This production was fraught with mishap. Georgia Hale (THE GOLD RUSH) could not, as originally planned, appear in this film. Chaplin's wife, Lita Grey, who was jealous of Hale, insisted that her childhood friend Merna Kennedy assume the role. During the course of the filming, the Chaplin-Grey marriage fell apart and, mindful of his experience with former wife Mildred whose lawyers tried to take possession of THE KID with a court order, Charlie took similar precautions by sending the unedited negatives of this film to New York. The action was well advised: Grey's attorneys attached his assets and placed his studio under guard until a divorce settlement could be reached. Among his other misfortunes, the circus tent was badly damaged in a storm, the entire set was later detroyed by a studio fire, and the circus wagons needed for one of the final scenes were stolen by student pranksters. Chaplin, who was disappointed in the first takes of the tightrope scenes, had taken a month to painstakingly reshoot the sequence, only to discover that the lab marred the negatives with scratches. On September 7, 1926 Chaplin closed his studio so he could be a pallbearer at Rudolph Valentino's funeral.

STARRING: Charles Chaplin, Merna Kennedy, Betty Morrisey, Harry Crocker
PRODUCER, DIRECTOR, WRITER: Charles Chaplin
PHOTOGRAPHER: Roland Totheroh
PICTURED: *Charles Chaplin*

CHARLIE CHAPLIN in "The CIRCUS"

UNITED ARTISTS PICTURE

High jinks on the high wire.

MARION DAVIES
in the Leap Year Picture
The Patsy
with
MARIE DRESSLER
LAWRENCE GRAY
Based on the play by Barry Connors. Continuity by Agnes Christine Johnston.
A KING VIDOR PRODUCTION
A MARION DAVIES PRODUCTION
Directed by KING VIDOR
A Metro-Goldwyn-Mayer PICTURE
LUBIN PUB. CO., N. Y.
MADE IN U. S. A.

THE PATSY

1928 · MGM

In this rollicking, energetic comedy, Davies delightfully impersonates screen stars Pola Negri, Mae Murray and Lillian Gish, and firmly established her talent as a comedienne. Marie Dressler plays her domineering mother. Louis B. Mayer appreciated the value of associating with newspaper magnate William Randolph Hearst — Davies' devoted patron and lover — both in terms of social prestige and free publicity for all MGM films. Mayer offered to finance her films, pay the star a weekly salary of $10,000, cut Hearst in on a share of the profits and provide a 14-room bungalow for Davies' use on the MGM lot. In 1934, because roles intended for Davies had been assigned instead to Thalberg's wife, Norma Shearer, Hearst cut his ties to MGM and moved the famous bungalow for a brief stay on the Warner's lot. The financial setbacks of the Hearst empire in 1937 hastened the end of Davies' film career, which had begun to decline with the advent of sound.

STARRING: Marion Davies, Orville Caldwell, Marie Dressler, Lawrence Gray, Jane Winton
DIRECTOR: King Vidor
SCENARIO: Agnes Christine Johnston, based on the play by Barry Connors
PICTURED: *Marion Davies, Jane Winton, Lawrence Gray*

THE CAMERAMAN

1928 · MGM

In this comedy, filmed on location in New York with the working title SNAP SHOTS, Keaton plays a street photographer who falls in love with Sally (Day), who works for the Hearst Newsreel. To win her, he becomes an apprentice cameraman. Intrigued by the artistic opportunities, Keaton triumphantly produces ludicrous reels of trick photography — horses galloping backwards over hurdles and a battleship that leaves the high seas to sail down the streets of New York. Among the perfectly realized gags in this masterpiece are Keaton playing a solitary game of baseball in an empty stadium, the Chinatown festival and fight in which he encourages the fighters, a monkey filming his rescue of a drowning girl, and his nonchalant acceptance of a hero's ticker-tape welcome intended for Charles Lindbergh. MGM reaped a rich harvest with their first Keaton feature, but from the beginning the new employee, accustomed to running his own show, chafed under the restrictions imposed by the studio process. In 1928 Joseph Schenck sold Keaton's contract to MGM in a deal that guaranteed the comedian $150,000 per picture, making him one of the top ten highest paid players at that studio. The move also robbed Keaton of artistic control over his work and marked the beginning of his decline. After he suggested the idea for this story, MGM writers presented him with an intricate plot and a multitude of characters that Keaton summarily threw out, claiming that the best comedies are simple. He infuriated Sedgwick with his pre-emptive behavior, but when the comedian sat back patiently waiting for instruction, the director was at a loss and finally permitted Keaton to work out his own comedy bits. Initially, Keaton had to persuade Thalberg to allow the company to film on location in New York, but when crowds mobbed them on the city's streets, he had to talk the studio chief into permitting them to return to MGM to complete their work on the backlot.

STARRING: Buster Keaton, Marceline Day, Harold Goodwin, Harry Gribbon, Sidney Bracy
PRODUCER: Lawrence Weingarten
DIRECTOR: Edward Sedgwick
SCENARIO: Richard Schayer
STORY: Clyde Bruckman, Lew Lipton
PICTURED: *Marceline Day, Buster Keaton*

A Metro-Goldwyn-Mayer PICTURE

BUSTER KEATON in THE CAMERAMAN

TINTYPES 10¢

"Hold that—and watch the birdie!"

MADE IN U. S. A.

HAL ROACH presents

STAN LAUREL • OLIVER HARDY
in
PERFECT DAY

PERFECT DAY

1929 · MGM-Hal Roach

It's a perfect day for a picnic, but everything goes awry as the boys and their wives, continually bidding goodbye, embark on their outing. After a series of hilarious mishaps, they're finally on their way, but as they cross a muddy pool, the family car sinks slowly in the seemingly bottomless puddle. As they disappear completely from view, they have one last chance to bid 'adieu.

STARRING: Stan Laurel, Oliver Hardy, Edgar Kennedy, Kay Deslys, Isabelle Keith
PRODUCER: Hal Roach
DIRECTOR: James Parrott
STORY: Hal Roach and Leo McCarey
STORY EDITOR: H.M. Walker
PICTURED: *Stan Laurel, Oliver Hardy, Kay Deslys, Isabelle Keith, Edgar Kennedy*

CITY LIGHTS

1931 · United Artists

This bittersweet masterpiece tells the tragic tale of a poor man (Chaplin) who falls in love with a blind flower girl (Cherrill) and, because of a chance meeting with an eccentric millionaire, is able to provide the funds necessary to restore her eyesight. The simple story of chance encounters leading to heart-wrenching outcomes begins with Chaplin climbing through a limousine snarled in a traffic jam and finding himself mistaken for a millionaire by the blind girl who hands him a flower. Chaplin later comes across a drunken suicidal millionaire bent on drowning himself in a river; his fickle generosity provides the poor man with the money necessary for the flower girl's operation. Unfortunately it also dooms him to imprisonment for theft. He discovers upon his release that the girl — her eyesight restored — is running a flower shop. While offering a coin to the pitiful tramp, she's bewildered to recognize him as her benefactor. Chaplin's social conscience is quietly revealed throughout this painstakingly constructed and simply played tragicomedy, but most overtly in the opening sequence. The unemployed man is discovered asleep in the lap of the newly unveiled Statue to Prosperity, a public monument solemnly guarded by armed officers. Although sound was available, Chaplin hated the new technology and opted for silence, orchestrating the picture with musical instruments and sound effects that mimicked the tinny, metallic sounds of early talkies.

For the first time Chaplin worked with a leading lady (Cherrill) for whom he had no personal feelings and that, plus her lack of previous acting experience and his perfectionist demands, caused considerable tension between them. Chaplin required her presence on set even though the actress sat idle for months on end during the two-year production schedule. At long last working in front of the camera, she enraged him one day by asking to leave early for a hair appointment. He fired her and then, after several attempts to replace the actress, was finally persuaded by his staff to rehire her — and did, after meeting Cherrill's demand to double her salary. Harry Myers stepped in to play the millionaire after Chaplin fired Henry Clive when the actor, recovering from bronchial illness, requested that his drowning scene be scheduled late in the day because the lake water would be warmer. Jean Harlow appears as an extra in the hilarious night club sequence.

STARRING: Charles Chaplin, Virginia Cherrill, Harry Myers, Hank Mann
PRODUCER, DIRECTOR, WRITER: Charles Chaplin
PHOTOGRAPHER: Roland Totheroh
ART DIRECTOR: Charles D. Hall
MUSIC: Charles Chaplin
MUSIC DIRECTOR: Alfred Newman
PICTURED: *Harry Myers, Charles Chaplin*

CHARLIE
CHAPLIN

CITY LIGHTS

UNITED ARTISTS PICTURE

WHEELER-WOOLSEY

DOROTHY LEE

"CAUGHT PLASTERED"

CAUGHT PLASTERED

1931 · RKO

Wheeler and Woolsey, RKO's premiere comedy team, aid an old woman with her failing drugstore and find themselves fighting a gang of burglars. The two comics appeared in the stage version of RIO RITA and when that production was filmed in 1929, they were signed to studio contracts. After making nearly 25 films together, the duo's career ended with Woolsey's sudden death from a kidney ailment in 1938. Douglas MacLean, who wrote and produced the film, had begun as a leading comedy star at Paramount in the '20s and switched careers when sound arrived. Jason Robards Sr., a prominent stage actor, appeared in more than 100 Hollywood films, starring in many silents.

STARRING: Bert Wheeler, Robert Woolsey, Dorothy Lee, Jason Robards Sr., Lucy Beaumont
ASSOCIATE PRODUCER: Douglas MacLean
DIRECTOR: William Seiter
STORY: Douglas MacLean
ADAPTATION AND DIAOGUE: Ralph Spence
PICTURED: *Bert Wheeler, Robert Woolsey, Jason Robards Sr., Lucy Beaumont*

PALMY DAYS

1931 · United Artists

In Cantor's fifth film and possibly his best, he's a stooge for a fake spiritualist with a fortune-telling racket. The former singing waiter with the inimitable voice — that later made him a radio star — and the rolling bug-eyes was a popular vaudeville comedian who made his film debut in the role he created in his Broadway hit KID BOOTS (1926). Another Broadway discovery, Busby Berkeley, had an impressive reputation as a theatrical director when Samuel Goldwyn signed him in 1930, and his work in several early films reveals a dependence on reliable stage routines. Long before he demonstrated his master's touch as an innovative choreographer of elaborate movie musicals, Berkeley displayed his string of Goldwyn Girls in typical chorus line-fashion using simple tricks to show off their legs. In the tracking shot for the "Bend Down, Sister" number, the dancers in turn lean forward in a rippling effect to display their cleavage for the camera — a technique Berkeley used in subsequent spectaculars. Broadway hoofer George Raft plays a henchman in one of his earliest screen appearances. Comedienne Greenwood, tall, energetic and kooky, was noted for her acrobatic dancing and high kicks.

STARRING: Eddie Cantor, Charlotte Greenwood, Barbara Weeks, Spencer Charters, Paul Page
PRODUCER: Samuel Goldwyn
DIRECTOR: Edward Sutherland
STORY AND DIALOGUE: Eddie Cantor, Morrie Ryskind, David Freedman
PICTURED: *Charlotte Greenwood, Eddie Cantor*

THE FOUR MARX BROTHERS

'MONKEY BUSINESS'

A Paramount Picture

MONKEY BUSINESS

1 9 3 1 · Paramount

As stowaways on a luxury liner, the Marx Brothers bring pandemonium aboard ship as they get mixed up with rival gangs — Groucho and Zeppo with one outfit and Harpo and Chico with the other — both involved with a kidnaping. Fast paced and maliciously wacky, the script gives all four a chance to impersonate fellow Paramount player Maurice Chevalier. Harpo is provided with a brilliantly imaginative sequence in which he takes refuge in a children's Punch 'n' Judy show and joins the act by clipping a pair of puppet legs to his collar like a necktie. For their first film written directly for the screen, they imported New York humorist S. J. Perelman who collaborated on this highly literate, verbally caustic script and stayed with them to co-write HORSEFEATHERS. The Marx Brothers were notoriously abusive to writers and made a point of never laughing at a story conference. Accordingly, Perelman recalled that at his first script meeting with them, they brought along a mob of girlfriends, dogs and gag writers to sit in and when the reading concluded, there was a long grim silence before Groucho said, "It stinks," and left.

STARRING: Groucho, Chico, Harpo, Zeppo, Thelma Todd, Rockliffe Fellowes, Ruth Hall, Tom Kennedy
DIRECTOR: Norman Z. McLeod
STORY: S. J. Perelman, Will B. Johnstone
ADDITIONAL DIALOGUE: Arthur Sheekman
PHOTOGRAPHY: Arthur L. Tod
PICTURED: *Groucho Marx, Rockliffe Fellowes*

BEAU HUNKS

1931 · MGM - Hal Roach

After Hardy is jilted by his girl, he and Laurel join the Foreign Legion and end up sharing barracks with several other soldiers jilted by the same woman. The boys redeem themselves in the eyes of their disapproving colonel (Middleton) by thwarting a tribal rebellion led by the villainous Abdul Kasim K'Horne (director Horne in a cameo role). Jean Harlow consented to having her photograph used as the love 'em and leave 'em seductress. Ex-Legionnaire Louis Van DeNecker served as technical advisor. Wearing heavy woolen uniforms and back packs in the grueling heat of the desert location left the company of actors with a variety of ailments including sunburn, blisters and eye injuries from the sandstorm sequence.

STARRING: Stan Laurel, Oliver Hardy, Charles Middleton, Charlie Hall, Stanley Sandford
PRODUCER: Hal Roach
DIRECTOR: James Horne
DIALOGUE: H. M. Walker
PHOTOGRAPHER: Art Lloyd, Jack Stevens
EDITOR: Richard Currier
SOUND: Elmer R. Raguse
PICTURED: *Oliver Hardy, Stan Laurel*

STAN LAUREL OLIVER HARDY IN BEAU HUNKS

Feminine technique was the same in King Arthur's days, if we can depend on Myrna Loy and Will Rogers' air of recognition.

WILL ROGERS
in
A CONNECTICUT
YANKEE
by MARK TWAIN
Directed by DAVID BUTLER

MADE IN U. S. A.

A CONNECTICUT YANKEE

1931 · Fox

The Connecticut yankee in King Arthur's court is the engaging and beloved Rogers playing the owner of a small town radio shop who is accidentally knocked unconscious by a blow on his head which transports him back to the time of the Knights of the Round Table. Rogers' version quickly strays from Mark Twain's story in this second of three screen adaptations of the book. Will's greatest gift to the court is the invention of the bathtub and, when the king wonders if people will want it, he's told they'll have to create a market for it by advertising. "Advertising is where you make people believe they must have something they've managed to do without all their lives." The actor, wit and homespun philosopher began his career as an entertainer twirling a rope in vaudeville. In his early days, the bashful Oklahoma cowboy kept a list of "Gags for Missing the Horse's Nose" in his back pocket to cover those occasional lulls in his act, for example: "Swingin' a rope's all right — if your neck ain't in it." Audiences howled and his fellow entertainers persuaded Rogers to incorporate more anecdotes and pithy one-liners into his routine. He drew much of his humorous commentary from the daily newspapers and soon became known as a political satirist — who was eventually proposed as a serious candidate for public office, including President of the United States. He declined to run for Governor of Oklahoma, but accepted a post as mayor of Beverly Hills. A delight to both co-workers and production chiefs, Rogers, who abhorred retakes, most often completed his films ahead of schedule, but was conscientious about paying the crew whatever salary was due them had they worked the full time. Having completed three films back-to-back, Rogers flew to Alaska with aviator Wiley Post and died in a plane crash August 15, 1935 at the age of 56.

STARRING: Will Rogers, Maureen O'Sullivan, Myrna Loy, Frank Albertson, William Farnum
DIRECTOR: David Butler
ADAPTATION AND DIALOGUE: William Conselman, Owen Davis, based on Mark Twain's story
PICTURED: *Will Rogers, Myrna Loy*

BROADMINDED

1931 · First National

In his eighth starring role for First National, the rubber-faced clown with the wide shovel-mouth is chased by Bela Lugosi in the role of Pancho, an irate South American whose hot dog is stolen by Brown. The plot is flimsy and the humor is belly-laugh broad, typical of Brown's appealing and wholesome comedy style. He projected an all-American, small town innocence in roles that cast him as the sweet, gullible underdog who wins the day with a show of spirited gumption. His screen personality reflected his humble Midwestern origins and Brown, who became an acrobat at nine, claimed he was the only little boy who ran away to join a circus with his family's blessings. He was also an avid athlete and a semi-pro baseball player with the unlikely distinction of being the only comedian after whom a baseball field is named. Well-loved and highly regarded throughout his long career, Brown is particularly remembered for his role in SOME LIKE IT HOT as Osgood Fielding, the wealthy dim-wit who falls for Jack Lemmon, a female impersonator in an all-girl band. Finally learning that the girl of his dreams is really a fella, Brown utters the film's famous closing line, "Well, nobody's perfect!" Todd, Brown's BROADMINDED co-star, was gifted with the rare combination of striking blonde beauty and superb comic skills. She appeared in approximately 120 films in her brief nine year career that ended abruptly in December of 1935 when she was found dead of carbon-monoxide poisoning in her parked car. The mystery of her tragic death — whether by suicide, accident or murder — at age 30 is still unsolved. Director Mervyn LeRoy sandwiched this comedy between his powerful social dramas, LITTLE CAESAR and I AM A FUGITIVE FROM A CHAIN GANG.

STARRING: Joe E. Brown, Ona Munson, William Collier, Jr., Marjorie White, Thelma Todd, Bela Lugosi
DIRECTOR: Mervyn LeRoy
SCREENPLAY: Bert Kalmer and Harry Ruby
PICTURED: *Joe E. Brown, Thelma Todd*

POLITICS

1931 · MGM

In her fifth teaming with comedienne Polly Moran, Dressler attempts to clean up crime in her home town by running for mayor and fighting gangsters infiltrating the city. Overweight and homely, Dressler made comedy her fortune and achieved her greatest stage success in 1910 playing a boardinghouse drudge in TILLIE'S NIGHTMARE. She was an international vaudeville headliner before Sennett brought her to Hollywood in 1914 at age 45 to star in his screen adaptation, TILLIE'S PUNCTURED ROMANCE, which became the first full-length comedy film. More films and stage work followed, but Dressler's career suffered a severe setback during the '20s for a variety of reasons. During the war years she'd put her career on hold to devote her energies to entertaining soldiers and selling Liberty Bonds, and then actively participated in an actors' labor dispute. Audience tastes had changed by the time she was prepared to resume her career and for nearly a decade Dressler struggled to support herself. She was a hostess in a New York supper club and contemplating a job as a housekeeper when friend and screenwriter Frances Marion served as the catalyst that eventually brought Dressler her screen triumphs. Marion had persuaded Thalberg to team Dressler and Moran in the raucous, brawling comedy THE CALLAHANS AND THE MURPHYS, a calamitous venture that deeply offended the Irish and marred her return to Hollywood. However, Marion's adaptation of O'Neill's classic ANNA CHRISTIE provided Dressler with the meaty role of the waterfront hag, Marthy, and her screenplay MIN AND BILL blessed the 60 year old comedienne with an Academy Award. She was a favorite of tyrannical MGM chief Louis B. Mayer and, while she was filming DINNER AT EIGHT with Jean Harlow, he succeeded for a time in protecting Dressler from learning that her ill health was caused by cancer, which soon claimed her life. Moran, her rough and rowdy co-star, is chiefly remembered for the six slapstick comedies they made together.

STARRING: Marie Dressler, Polly Moran, Karen Morley, William Bakewell, Roscoe Ates
DIRECTOR: Charles Reisner
SCREENPLAY: Wells Root, Malcolm Stuart Boylan, Zelda Sears
PICTURED: *Polly Moran, Marie Dressler*

MOVIE CRAZY

1932 · Paramount

Under the impression that he's been offered a studio screen test, small-town bumpkin Lloyd heads for Hollywood seeking fame and fortune. He's a washout as a suave leading man, but in the end his bumbling antics earn him a contract as a comedian. Woven throughout this comedy is a curious romance with enchanting screen actress Cummings, whom he woos as both a pretty, young starlet and an exotic Latin leading lady before it's revealed she's one and the same woman. In the hilarious coat gag, Lloyd discovers that in the men's room he's accidentally exchanged jackets with a magician. He returns to the elegant party and while dancing with the studio chief's wife (Hale), the magical contents of Lloyd's jacket — eggs, laundry, a bird, a rabbit, white mice and a boutonniere squirting water — sustain a classic gag sequence. Lloyd's foray into talking pictures with the cumbersome WELCOME DANGER (1929) wasn't a critical success and his thin, rather prissy voice was not an asset in the new medium. However, Lloyd endeavored to win back his huge '20s audience by fashioning a sound film that incorporated long silent sequences comprising the physical comedy and visual gags that had been his strength before talkies. Lloyd customarily used the reactions of preview audiences to further edit his films and, in this instance, he showed MOVIE CRAZY to a group of deaf people who reportedly were baffled only twice during the picture. The comedy was well made and garnered Lloyd's best reviews for a talkie but, perhaps because it was released at the height of the Depression, it did not fare well at the box office. Arthur Housman, one of the screen's most familiar drunks, plays the guest who's presented with the magician's white rabbit on his dinner plate.

STARRING: Harold Lloyd, Constance Cummings, Kenneth Thomson, Louise Closser Hale, Arthur Housman
PRODUCER: Harold Lloyd
DIRECTOR: Clyde Bruckman
STORY: Agnes Christine Johnston, John Grey, Felix Adler
SCREENPLAY AND DIALOGUE: Vincent Lawrence
PHOTOGRAPHER: Walter Lundin
PICTURED: *Arthur Housman, Harold Lloyd, Louise Closser Hale*

STAN **LAUREL** OLIVER **HARDY**

IN

PACK UP YOUR TROUBLES

A Metro-Goldwyn-Mayer PICTURE

COUNTRY OF ORIGIN U.S.A.

PACK UP YOUR TROUBLES

1932 · MGM-Hal Roach

Laurel and Hardy join the army when war is declared and end up capturing a brigade of German soldiers. After the armistice, the pair try to locate the relatives of a little girl (Lyn) whose father was a buddy who died in the war. Their only clue in the search is the last name "Smith." The enchanting three-year-old Lyn caught Roach's eye when she appeared in a Marie Dressler feature. Director Marshall stepped in to play the camp cook when the actor hired for the role didn't show up, and Laurel extended the director's screentime by improvising his appearance in a jail scene. Leo McCarey's younger brother Raymond had previously directed only one Laurel and Hardy short, and it's questionable whether the extent of his involvement in this feature entitled him to the co-directing credit he's given.

STARRING: Stan Laurel, Oliver Hardy, Donald Dillaway, Tom Kennedy, Grady Sutton, Jacqui Lyn, James Finlayson
PRODUCER: Hal Roach
DIRECTOR: George Marshall and Raymond McCarey
DIALOGUE: H.M. Walker
PHOTOGRAPHER: Art Lloyd
EDITOR: Richard Currier
SOUND: James Green
PICTURED: *Oliver Hardy, Stan Laurel, James Mason*

HORSEFEATHERS

1932 · Paramount

In this satire on the Depression, sports and education, Groucho, as Professor Quincy Adams Wagstaff, leads a university to ruin as its new president while Zeppo, as his student son, woos the luscious campus vamp (Todd). Chico, the local bootlegger, and Harpo, serving as a dogcatcher, are also enrolled as students simply to play football. In a cascade of biting foolery — when Harpo enrolls he signs his name with an "X" — the film pokes fun at the college mania for producing winning sports teams and serves as a general indictment of social values. Harpo, who played the sweet and mischievious mute in the Marx Brothers' comedies, had only a second-grade education. He claimed he quit school because a bully repeatedly dropped him out of a second-floor classroom window and he tired of explaining to the teacher how he'd left the room without permission.

STARRING: Groucho, Chico, Harpo, Zeppo, Thelma Todd, David Landau, Nat Pendleton
DIRECTOR: Norman Z. McLeod
STORY: Bert Kalmar, Harry Ruby, S. J. Perelman
PICTURED: *E.J. LeSaint, Groucho Marx, E.H. Calvert*

JEAN HARLOW · LEE TRACY

BLONDE BOMBSHELL

BOMBSHELL

1933 · MGM

In a scathing sendup of the movie business, Harlow is a film star longing for motherhood and a normal life while surrounded by the shallow, exploitive, egotistical denizens of Hollywood. Among the hangers-on is her unscrupulous press agent (Tracy) who foils her every attempt to achieve a cozy, ordinary life. Tracy and O'Brien, two of the screen's fastest-talking actors, appear together in this picture, with Tracy winning the honors for speediest delivery. Known for his hard-boiled cop and priest roles, the popular Irishman O'Brien made a total of five pictures in 1933. Morgan was a key supporting player in dozens of MGM films and is probably best remembered for his title role in THE WIZARD OF OZ. A former race car driver who got his start in films with Douglas Fairbanks, Fleming directed two of the screen's great classics, THE WIZARD OF OZ and GONE WITH THE WIND; for the latter he won an Academy Award.

STARRING: Jean Harlow, Lee Tracy, Frank Morgan, Franchot Tone, Pat O'Brien, Una Merkel
PRODUCER: Hunt Stromberg
DIRECTOR: Victor Fleming
SCREENPLAY: John Lee Mahin, Jules Furthman, from the play by Caroline Francke and Mack Crane
PICTURED: *Jean Harlow, Frank Morgan, Ted Healy*

THE BARBER SHOP

1933 · Paramount

When a customer inquires about a dog sitting by the barber chair, Fields says, "It's a funny thing about that dog. One day I was shaving a man and cut his ear off, and the dog got it. Been back here ever since." In his fourth and last short produced by Sennett, before Fields moved on to feature work, he has marital problems with his vegetarian wife (Cavanna) and to soothe his nerves, he plays a bass fiddle named Lena. Among the comic highlights is a scene where a cello gives birth to a litter of baby cellos and another where an obese man shrinks to midget size in a steamroom. After running away from home at age eleven, William Claude Dukenfield set out to become the world's greatest juggler. By age 20 he was a vaudeville headliner, soon to star on Broadway and give a command performance at Buckingham Palace. He made his film debut in the 1915 short THE POOL SHARK, but continued his stage career for another decade before D.W. Griffith directed him in a screen adaptation of his Broadway hit POPPY, retitled SALLY OF THE SAWDUST. Fields' unique comic persona — suspicious, misanthropic conman with a complete distrust of authority — owed much to the bitter heritage of his harsh, brutal childhood. The attitudes he expressed onscreen very much represented his offscreen personality as well. Because he distrusted banks and bankers, Fields squirreled his savings into as many as 700 small accounts in towns and cities as he was touring throughout the country, each under a different fictitious name. With the introduction of talkies, Fields' brand of verbal humor, delivered in his unique raspy-voiced throw-away style, made him a major comic star.

STARRING: W. C. Fields, Elise Cavanna, Harry Watson, Dagmar Oakland, Frank Yaconelli
PRODUCER: Mack Sennett
DIRECTOR: Arthur Ripley
SCREENPLAY: W. C. Fields
PICTURED: *Frank Yaconelli, W. C. Fields*

THE FOUR MARX BROTHERS IN 'Duck Soup'

Directed by LEO McCAREY

A Paramount Picture

"COUNTRY OF ORIGIN U.S.A." COPYRIGHT 1933 BY PARAMOUNT PICTURES DISTRIBUTING CORP.

THIS LOBBY DISPLAY LEASED FROM PARAMOUNT PICTURES DISTRIBUTING CORP.

DUCK SOUP

1933 · Paramount

Now recognized as the Marx Brothers' most striking film, it's a savage, biting satire on war and facism. With Groucho as President Rufus T. Firefly of Freedonia ("the land of the free") and Harpo and Chico as his spies, politics, government and international diplomacy are reduced to comic absurdity. Every function of government is lampooned, including the very serious business of war. A breach of etiquette compels Sylvania to declare war on Freedonia, with the monumental confrontation resulting in, among other things, musical mayhem running the gamut from opera to jazz to square dancing. Groucho's parliament unifies in a singing, dancing chorus to perform "All God's Chillun Got Guns." Harpo ridicules the patriotic fervor of Paul Revere in a provocative sequence of sexual innuendo in which he seduces a lush beauty — after which, first a pair of high heeled shoes, then Harpo's boots and finally a set of horseshoes are revealed. Wielding a pair of scissors, the manic, irrepressible Harpo emasculates neckties and chops off hair, cigars, sausages and coattails. When Freedonia achieves victory and wealthy matron Dumont bursts into a heartfelt chorus of "Hail Freedonia," the brothers pelt her with fruit. In the inspired mirror scene, Groucho and Harpo, dressed in matching white nightgowns and caps, ape each other's movements as though looking at a reflection — with Chico arriving to add to the silliness. This unrelieved comic assault was originally called CRACKED ICE, but the title was changed to conform with the menagerie of names preceding it: ANIMAL CRACKERS, MONKEY BUSINESS and HORSEFEATHERS. Title not withstanding, critics and audiences alike originally considered the picture a dog. It was the most expensive to date of Paramount's productions and its poor performance at the boxoffice prompted the studio to drop the Marxes' contract. Their move to MGM cost them the accomplished writing team of social satirists who had provided the ruthless, iconoclastic context for their comedy. It was also the end of the line for Zeppo who, tired of playing the parody of the romantic juvenile, left the trio to carry on without him while he became a theatrical agent with Frank Orsatti's office. The Marx Brothers satires, attacking every discontent of the day, touched raw nerve and were taken seriously in some quarters, indicated by Benito Mussolini's condemnation of the Marx Brothers in 1939 when he ordered his countrymen not to watch them.

STARRING: Groucho, Chico, Harpo, Zeppo, Raquel Torres, Margaret Dumont, Louis Calhern
DIRECTOR: Leo McCarey
STORY, LYRICS, MUSIC: Bert Kalmer, Harry Ruby
ADDITIONAL DIALOGUE: Arthur Sheekman, Nat Perrin
PICTURED: *Harpo, Chico, Zeppo, Groucho*

INTERNATIONAL HOUSE

1933 · Paramount

An offbeat, delightful hodgepodge of comedy and musical numbers (such as Calloway singing "Reefer Man") in which Fields, the master of florid rhetoric, plays the crazy inventor of the "radioscope." The auction of this early television invention attracts an assortment of eccentric bidders from all over the world to a Chinese hotel managed by Pangborn. Joyce, playing herself, makes life miserable for Lugosi, cast as a Russian general convinced that the actress is dallying with Fields. A host of radio personalities — Vallee, Col. Stoopnagle and Budd, and Baby Rose Marie — are worked into the plot, with Burns and Allen playing a doctor and nurse. A satire on MGM's hit GRAND HOTEL, this Paramount release was one of a series of all-star movies that came to be known as "clambakes". Fields especially appealed to the post-Prohibition audience, in sympathy with his desire for alcohol, and his performance was singled out by Time magazine as "a private spree."

STARRING: W.C. Fields, Peggy Hopkins Joyce, Stu Erwin, Sari Maritza, George Burns, Gracie Allen, Bela Lugosi, Franklin Pangborn, Rudy Vallee, Sterling Holloway, Cab Calloway, Baby Rose Marie
PRODUCER: Albert Lewis
DIRECTOR: Edward Sutherland
STORY: Neil Brant, Louis E. Heifetz
SCREENPLAY: Frances Martin, Walter DeLeon
PICTURED: *Lumsden Hare, Franklin Pangborn, George Burns, Gracie Allen, Stu Erwin, W. C. Fields, Sari Maritza, Bela Lugosi*

'INTERNATIONAL HOUSE.

SPIRIT
OF
SOUTH BROOKLYN

WITH
**PEGGY HOPKINS
JOYCE**

W.C.FIELDS

RUDY VALLEE

STUART ERWIN

GEORGE BURNS
and
GRACIE ALLEN

**Col.STOOPNAGLE
and BUDD**

CAB CALLOWAY
AND HIS ORCHESTRA

A
Paramount
Picture

"SIX OF A KIND"

WITH
Charlie **RUGGLES**
Mary **BOLAND**
W.C. **FIELDS**
Alison **SKIPWORTH**
George **BURNS**
and Gracie **ALLEN**

Directed by
LEO McCAREY

A Paramount Picture

SIX OF A KIND

1934 · Paramount

This zany comedy features an abundance of superb talents in a story about Ruggles and Boland, who invite Burns and Allen along for companionship, on a cross-country second honeymoon. Fields, as Sheriff John Hoxley is again paired with English character actress Skipworth, best remembered for the three films in which she plays his indomitable foil. Fields, relegated to a secondary role, nevertheless has the opportunity to display his celebrated billiards routine and elaborate at length on how he acquired the nickname Honest John. Burns and Allen, who married in 1926 and appeared in a total of eighteen shorts and feature films together, were an enduring comedy team on stage, screen, radio and television until Gracie's death in 1964. After a 35 year absence from the screen, Burns made a triumphant Oscar-winning return in THE SUNSHINE BOYS (1975). Genial character comedian Ruggles was often the henpecked screen husband of madcap, scatterbrain Boland.

STARRING: Charles Ruggles, Mary Boland, W. C. Fields, Alison Skipworth, George Burns, Gracie Allen
DIRECTOR: Leo McCarey
STORY: Keene Thompson, Douglas MacLean
SCREENPLAY: Walter DeLeon, Harry Ruskin
PICTURED: *W.C. Fields, Mary Boland, Gracie Allen*

JIMMY THE GENT

1934 · Warner Bros.

A bouncy, lickety-split comedy in which fast talking crooked businessman Cagney cleans up his act to impress Davis. Specializing in fake inheritance claims, he manufactures fictitious heirs to unclaimed fortunes. Spinning in a world of conmen who'll do anything for a buck, the impressionable Davis is taken in by their "refined society manners" — such as serving high tea in the office.

STARRING: James Cagney, Bette Davis, Alice White, Allen Jenkins, Philip Reed, Mayo Methot, Alan Dinehart
EXECUTIVE PRODUCER: Jack L. Warner
DIRECTOR: Michael Curtiz
SCREENPLAY: Bertram Milhauser
ORIGINAL STORY: Laird Doyle and Ray Nazarro
PICTURED: *Bette Davis, James Cagney, Allen Jenkins, Alan Dinehart*

W. C. FIELDS

IN

"You're Telling Me"

WITH LARRY 'BUSTER' CRABBE • JOAN MARSH • ADRIENNE AMES
DIRECTED BY ERLE C. KENTON

a Paramount Picture

YOU'RE TELLING ME

1934 · Paramount

To demonstrate his latest invention, a puncture-proof tire, Fields is wearing a catcher's mitt to retrieve a spent bullet after it bounces off the tire. A remake of Fields' SO'S YOUR OLD MAN (1926), this film so closely follows the original that in several instances silent titles are incorporated into the sound dialogue. The silent, however, featured an unbreakable windshield instead of the puncture-proof tire. Olympic gold medal swimming champion Crabbe (1932) had entered films the year before with a role in an action-adventure tale, a juvenile lead in a college romance and his first feature and serial versions of the Tarzan stories. In this film he plays the rich boyfriend of Fields' daughter.

STARRING: W. C. Fields, Joan Marsh, Larry "Buster" Crabbe, Adrienne Ames
PRODUCER: William LeBaron
DIRECTOR: Erle C. Kenton
SCREENPLAY: Walter DeLeon, Paul M. Jones
STORY: Julian Street
DIALOGUE: J.P. McEvoy
PICTURED: *Jerry Stewart, W. C. Fields, George Irving*

A NIGHT AT THE OPERA

1935 · MGM

Irving Thalberg, a bridge-playing crony of Chico's, wisely hired the trio (Zeppo had left the group to become a theatrical agent) in 1933 after Paramount had dropped their contract. Wiser still, the legendary production chief of MGM sent the brothers on the road with a pack of writers to hone the script in front of a live audience. It was well worth the effort. Critics and audiences alike considered the team washed up after the poorly received DUCK SOUP. Despite this low ebb, the brothers negotiated an astounding contract guaranteeing them 15% of the gross receipts. Thalberg did his utmost to ensure success by providing the Marx Brothers with proven comedy screenwriter Ryskind, collaborating with celebrated playwright Kaufman, and by hiring burly gag-smith Al Boasberg, credited with supplying the famous crowded-stateroom scene. Favorite foils Dumont and Rumann were brought in, and singers Carlisle and Jones were cast as the romantic duo. At first the two were revoiced by Metropolitan Opera stars but in the end, their own fine singing voices prevailed. Still thoroughly destructive of social convention and personal property, the Marx Brothers retained their iconoclastic lunacy through this picture; however, it marked the beginning of their considerable decline into film mediocrity. The movie made a $3,000,000 profit and won almost unanimous critical praise.

STARRING: Groucho, Chico, Harpo, Kitty Carlisle, Allan Jones, Margaret Dumont, Siegfried Rumann
PRODUCER: Irving Thalberg
DIRECTOR: Sam Wood
STORY: James Kevin McGuinness
SCREENPLAY: George S. Kaufman, Morrie Ryskind
ADDITIONAL MATERIAL: Al Boasberg
PHOTOGRAPHY: Merritt B. Gerstad
ART DIRECTION: Cedric Gibbons, Ben Carre and Edwin B. Willis
EDITING: William LeVanway
MUSIC: Herbert Stothart
PICTURED: *Groucho, Walter Woolf King, Harpo*

GROUCHO CHICO · HARPO
MARX BROTHERS

A NIGHT AT THE OPERA

"So you think you have me at your mercy, you cad!"

A Metro-Goldwyn-Mayer PICTURE

"COUNTRY OF ORIGIN U.S.A."

ADOLPH ZUKOR presents

"RUGGLES of RED GAP"

WITH

CHARLES LAUGHTON

MARY BOLAND

CHARLIE RUGGLES

ZASU PITTS

ROLAND YOUNG

LEILA HYAMS

Directed by Leo McCarey

A PARAMOUNT PICTURE

RUGGLES OF RED GAP

1 9 3 5 · Paramount

In Laughton's finest comedy performance, he plays a butler won in a poker game by Western rube Ruggles and his social-climbing wife Boland, with Pitts as the spinster who catches his eye. An enormous hit, this film secured McCarey's reputation as a brilliant comedy director who infused his work with a blend of explosive humor and unabashed sentimentality. A law school graduate, McCarey abandoned his legal career to work as an assistant to director Tod Browning in 1920 at the age of 22. He honed his writing and directing skills with Roach, working primarily with Laurel and Hardy, and went on to direct Lloyd, the Marx Brothers (DUCK SOUP) and W. C. Fields (SIX OF A KIND). RUGGLES OF RED GAP had been filmed in 1918 and 1923 — and it was later remade as FANCY PANTS (1950) with Bob Hope and Lucille Ball — but McCarey made it his own. In an enchanting scene of romantic intoxication, Lord Burnstead (Young), newly arrived from England, is entertained by Nell Kenner (Hyams) at her parlor piano. In a wide ranging film career, Laughton created three of his most memorable roles in 1935: in addition to RUGGLES, he played Javert in LES MISERABLES and Captain Bligh in MUTINY ON THE BOUNTY.

STARRING: Charles Laughton, Mary Boland, Charles Ruggles, Zasu Pitts, Roland Young, Leila Hyams
PRODUCER: Arthur Hornblow, Jr.
DIRECTOR: Leo McCarey
SCREENPLAY: Walter DeLeon, Harlan Thomson, Humphrey Pearson; adapted from the play and novel by Harry Leon Wilson
PICTURED: *Zasu Pitts, Charles Laughton*

HOI POLLOI

1935 · Columbia

Two professors argue the possibilities of making a gentleman out of anyone and wager $10,000 on the results; the Three Stooges are chosen as subjects for the experiment. During an elaborate dinner party in their honor to celebrate the apparent success of the ruffians' transformation, the Stooges revert to type and reduce the party to shambles. This story was remade as HALF-WITS HOLIDAY (1947) and PIES AND GUYS (1958) — stock footage and various gags were also recycled. Specializing in prankish, vulgar slapstick, the Stooges brutally kicked, gouged, bopped, bullied, and tweaked one another's noses in some 200 shorts for Columbia between 1934 and 1958. Brothers Moe and Shemp Howard had formed a vaudeville team in 1923 to play second bananas to comedian Ted Healy. Larry Fine joined the brothers in 1928 and the trio supported Healy in their feature debut SOUP TO NUTS (1930). Curly replaced his brother Shemp, and the Stooges embarked on the longest running series of two-reelers in the history of sound films. When Curly left in 1946, Shemp returned to take his place. When Shemp died in 1955, Joe Besser stepped in, to be followed by Joe ("Curly Joe") De Rita.

STARRING: Moe, Larry, Curly, Harry Holmes, Bud Jamison
DIRECTOR: Del Lord
SCREENPLAY: Felix Adler
PICTURED: *Curly Howard, Betty McMahon, Moe Howard, Phyllis Crane, Larry Fine*

MOE · CURLY · LARRY
3 STOOGES
in
HALF
SHOT
SHOOTERS
COLUMBIA PICTURES
A COLUMBIA 2 REEL COMEDY
This advertising is the property of Columbia Pictures Corporation and is leased pursuant to an agreement for use only in connection with the exhibition of the above motion picture and prohibiting its sub-lease or resale.
PRINTED IN U. S. A.
Copyrighted by Columbia Pictures Corp., New York, N. Y., 1936

HALF SHOT SHOOTERS

1936 · Columbia

The Stooges, discharged from the Army after World War I, accidentally re-up years later while unemployed. In typical stooge fashion, they prematurely fire a cannon and sink an admiral's flagship. Mysteriously this short subject, as well as the earlier HOI POLLOI, were banned in Holland.

STARRING: Moe, Larry, Curly, Stanley Blystone, Vernon Dent
ASSOCIATE PRODUCER: Jules White
DIRECTOR: Preston Black
STORY AND SCREENPLAY: Clyde Bruckman
PICTURED: *Curly, Moe, Larry, Vernon Dent*

THE BOHEMIAN GIRL

1936 · MGM-Hal Roach

A charming blend of comedy, romance and music, this bucolic operetta was the first of two Laurel and Hardy features released in 1936. The two bumbling pickpockets are members of a gypsy caravan encamped in the woods of Count Arnheim (Carlton), whose daughter Aline (Hood), wearing an identifying medallion, scampers away from the palace one day and is lost. She's "adopted" by Hardy's wife (Busch) who presents him with the child, saying "I didn't want her to know who her father was until she was old enough to stand the shock." When Hardy's wife runs off with her current lover Devilshoof (Moreno), he and Stan are left to raise the abandoned girl. Twelve years later, when the caravan is once more encamped in the Count's woods, the young woman is reunited with her father in storybook fashion. Five-year-old Our Gang leading lady Darla Hood played the child in the early sequences, with Jacqueline Wells (who later changed her name to Julie Bishop) playing Aline as a young woman. One of the most memorable scenes displays Laurel's pantomime talents as he becomes steadily more inebriated while bottling wine. The operetta also contains Balfe's best known song, "I Dreamt I Dwelt in Marble Halls." As originally filmed, Moreno (the silent screen idol who was Garbo's leading man in THE TEMPTRESS) dallied with Todd, the gypsy queen's daughter. Five days after the first preview, Thelma Todd was found dead in her car, asphyxiated by carbon-monoxide fumes. Concerned about the public's response to her death, Roach and Laurel reworked many of her scenes. In Germany the Nazi Party banned the film because it portrayed gypsies as "acceptable."

STARRING: Stan Laurel, Oliver Hardy, Thelma Todd, Jacqueline Wells, James Finlayson, Mae Busch, Antonio Moreno, Darla Hood, William P. Carlton
PRODUCER: Hal Roach
DIRECTOR: James Horne, Charles Rogers
SCREENPLAY: Comedy version of the 1843 opera by Michael W. Balfe
PHOTOGRAPHY: Art Lloyd and Francis Colby
EDITING: Bert Jordan, Louis McManus
SOUND: Elmer R. Raguse
MUSICAL DIRECTION: Nathaniel Shilkret
PICTURED: *Sam Lufkin, Stan Laurel, Oliver Hardy*

A Metro-Goldwyn-Mayer
PICTURE

"I told you I'd get his
money — it's the gypsy
in me!"

STAN   OLIVER
LAUREL-HARDY
in The BOHEMIAN GIRL

COUNTRY OF ORIGIN U. S. A.

William
POWELL · Carole
LOMBARD
in
My Man
Godfrey

WITH

ALICE   GAIL   JEAN
BRADY · PATRICK · DIXON

Based on the novel by Eric Hatch · Screenplay by Morrie Ryskind and Eric Hatch · Directed by Gregory La Cava

CHAS. R. ROGERS
EXECUTIVE PRODUCER
A UNIVERSAL PICTURE

MY MAN GODFREY

1936 · Universal

As *Variety* reported in 1936, "Lombard has played screwball dames before, but none so screwy as this one. From start to finish, with no letdowns or lapses into quiet sanity..." The *New York Times* described Lombard's character as "a one-track mind with grass growing over its rails." In fact, this film presented an entire family of screwballs. Thinking he's a tramp who needs a job, the wealthy, eccentric Bullock family hire Godfrey Parke (Powell) as a butler after daughter Irene (Lombard) picks him up in a scavanger hunt at the city dump. In the end, the "forgotten man" Godfrey turns out to be both wealthy and socially conscious, and becomes the salvation of the Bullock family. It was at Powell's insistence that Lombard — his wife from 1931 to 1933 — play opposite him in this, their third and last film together. A child actress, Lombard had appeared in knockabout Sennett comedies at 19, graduated to routine roles in features, and finally emerged a star at 26 opposite John Barrymore in TWENTIETH CENTURY. Beloved by co-workers and adored by her legion of fans, Lombard died tragically in a 1942 air crash while touring the Midwest to sell U.S. war bonds. Ryskind collaborated with George S. Kaufman on a number of musical comedies, sharing a Pulitzer Prize with Kaufman and Ira Gershwin for OF THEE I SING, and wrote several of the Marx Brothers screen comedies.

STARRING: William Powell, Carole Lombard, Alice Brady, Gail Patrick, Jean Dixon, Eugene Pallette, Alan Mowbray, Mischa Auer
PRODUCER: Gregory LaCava
DIRECTOR: Gregory LaCava
SCREENPLAY: Morrie Ryskind, Eric Hatch, based on the Eric Hatch novel
PICTURED: *Carole Lombard, William Powell*

WAY OUT WEST

1937 · MGM - Hal Roach

Laurel and Hardy are sent to deliver a dead prospector friend's gold-mine deed to his daughter (Lawrence); however, villainous saloon owner Mickey Finn (Finlayson) sidetracks them to the wrong girl, his wife Lola (Lynne). The deed is grabbed, retrieved, snatched and recovered in a variety of comic turns. When he's reminded of his pledge to eat Hardy's hat if they didn't recover the deed, Laurel at first cries, then nibbles apprehensively and finally salts the bowler and eats with gusto. Hardy succumbs to this display and surrepticiously takes a bite of the hat, finding his bowler nowhere near as tasty a treat as Laurel has. Each time they cross the stream on the outskirts of Brushwood Gulch, Hardy disappears into the same pothole. There are several delightful musical numbers in this western yarn, with Chill Wills and the Avalon Boys' Quartet as backups, and the film earned an Oscar nomination for best music scoring. Bald and sporting a mustache, Finlayson, the Scotsman known as Fin, possessed a rare gift for the effective "double-take" and "fadeaway". Though he longed for stardom, Fin remained a superb character actor and supporting player who is best known for his work in a succession of Laurel and Hardy films.

STARRING: Stan Laurel, Oliver Hardy, James Finlayson, Sharon Lynne, Rosina Lawrence,
PRODUCER: Stan Laurel
DIRECTOR: James Horne
ORIGINAL STORY: Jack Jevne, Charles Rogers
SCREENPLAY: Charles Rogers, Felix Adler, James Parrott
PICTURED: *Stan Laurel, Oliver Hardy*

"Call the fire department—
my thumb's ablaze!"

Stan **LAUREL** Oliver **HARDY** in **WAY OUT WEST**

A Metro-Goldwyn-Mayer PICTURE

COUNTRY OF ORIGIN U. S. A.

A DAY AT THE RACES

1937 · MGM

Groucho is Dr. Hugo Z. Hackenbush, the medic summoned to treat hypochondriac Dumont, Groucho's favorite target for insults. This was the final Marx brothers comedy effort before their films were overwhelmed by musical numbers and romantic subplots. As with A NIGHT AT THE OPERA, the comedy team and a host of writers went on the road to audience-test the gags, traveling 6000 miles and passing out 30,000 comment cards. The film earned $4,000,000 at the boxoffice, but suffered from mixed notices because of the variety-act formula: production numbers interspersed with comedy bits. The scathing social comment and reckless bawdiness of the earlier Marx Brothers films was missing. Irving Thalberg, the brilliant 37-year-old MGM production chief, an avid supporter of the Marx brothers, died during the filming. George S. Kaufman returned to Broadway and, of the other wits and social satirists who collaborated on previous Marx Brothers films, only gagman Boasberg remained on board. With stuffy aplomb, Dumont became the doyenne of seven Marx Brothers films after first joining the brothers in their zany stage comedies.

STARRING: Groucho, Chico, Harpo, Allan Jones, Maureen O'Sullivan, Margaret Dumont, Siegfried Rumann
PRODUCER: Irving G. Thalberg and Sam Wood
DIRECTOR: Sam Wood
ASSOCIATE PRODUCER: Max Siegel
STORY: Robert Pirosh, George Seaton
SCREENPLAY: Robert Pirosh, George Seaton, George Oppenheimer
PICTURED: *Groucho, Esther Muir, Chico, Harpo*

TOPPER

1937 · MGM - Hal Roach

W hile speeding down a country road, the young, attractive and very much in love George and Marion Kirby (Grant and Bennett) are killed instantly when their car hits a tree — hardly a promising start to a comedy. However, as described by the *New York Times* critic of the day, Frank S. Nugent, "the ectoplasmic screwballs" rise from the wreckage of their sports car to contemplate their rich, frivolous life style and determine to do one good deed before passing into the hereafter: to save the timorous, henpecked Topper (Roland) from his stuffy, humdrum existence. The high-spirited couple, invisible to everyone but Topper, spin the staid milquetoast into the glittering world of the nightclub set as his befuddled wife (Burke) looks on with growing alarm. Once Dr. Watson to John Barrymore's Sherlock Holmes, Young firmly established his screen personality with a series of whimsical, bemused characters — most notably Topper, which earned him an Oscar nomination in 1937. The stylish, husky voiced Bennett and the dashingly handsome Grant are a perfect blend of the wit and elegance that are the underpinnings of '30s screwball comedy. Burke, once the the toast of Broadway and the wife of Florenz Ziegfeld, embarked on a second Hollywood career after his death in 1932 and delighted audiences as a feather-brained, fluttery voiced character actress.

STARRING: Constance Bennett, Cary Grant, Roland Young, Billie Burke, Alan Mowbray, Hedda Hopper, Eugene Pallette
PRODUCER: Hal Roach
DIRECTOR: Norman Z. McLeod
SCREENPLAY: Jack Jevne, Eric Hatch, Eddie Moran, from the Thorne Smith novel *The Jovial Ghosts*
PICTURED: *Constance Bennett, Cary Grant, Roland Young*

"Strange attitude... for a banker!"

HAL ROACH presents

Constance BENNETT

Cary GRANT

IN

TOPPER

A Metro-Goldwyn-Mayer PICTURE

COUNTRY OF ORIGIN U. S. A.

THE AWFUL TRUTH

1937 · Columbia

An enormous critical and boxoffice success nominated for five Academy Awards, this is the picture Cary Grant tried everything to avoid doing. Simply, the plot revolved around the Warriners (Grant and Dunne), who separate because of jealousy and misunderstanding, then wickedly scheme to outwit and sabotage each other's subsequent romances only to reunite in the end. Now recognized as the definitive screwball comedy and Grant's breakthrough film, during his early days on the movie the actor was convinced he was making a fool of himself. He tried to persuade his friend Joel McCrea to replace him, begged Ralph Bellamy (playing Daniel Leeson, Dunne's rich Oklahoma oilman) to switch roles, and attempted to barter with Columbia's Harry Cohn to let him out of the picture. There was no script; director McCarey is said to have improvised scenes with screenwriter Delmar in a parked car on Hollywood Boulevard, arriving on the set with scrap-paper notes in his pockets, then playing the piano until inspiration struck. It did, and McCarey won an Oscar for the sparkling comedy that he completed in just six weeks. Bellamy, who was nominated for his supporting role, reported for his first day on the picture with no idea of the role he was to play and went on camera wearing the clothes he'd worn to the studio. With his own fine pedigree in screwball comedy, Mr. Smith, the canine subject of the Warriner's custody battle, had previously appeared as Nick and Nora's Asta in MGM's THIN MAN films, and went on to play George in BRINGING UP BABY.

STARRING: Irene Dunne, Cary Grant, Ralph Bellamy, Alex D'Arcy, Cecil Cunningham
PRODUCER: Leo McCarey
DIRECTOR: Leo McCarey
ASSOCIATE PRODUCER: Everett Riskin
SCREENPLAY: Vina Delmar, based on the 1922 play by Arthur Richman
PICTURED: *Ralph Bellamy, Irene Dunne, Esther Dale, Cary Grant*

BLUEBEARD'S EIGHTH WIFE

1 9 3 8 · P a r a m o u n t

French girl Nicole de Loiselle (Colbert), daughter of impoverished nobleman Marquis de Loiselle (Horton), becomes the eighth and final bride of seven-times-divorced millionaire Michael Brandon (Cooper). In this love and money comedy, boy meets girl in a department store: down to earth Nicole offers to buy pajama bottoms so playboy Brandon can buy the tops. When he tries to seduce her by plying her with alcohol, the savvy Nicole, knowing Brandon is violently allergic to onions, swallows a mouthful of scallions and breathes the noxious fumes in his face as he kisses her. She literally drives him crazy and he ends up strait-jacketed in a loony bin. Along the way she marries him, divorces him, collects a $100,000 a year settlement and returns to him — all in true screwball fashion. This was Lubitsch's second film (the first was ANGEL with Marlene Dietrich) after his brief stint as Paramount production chief and, because the two films fared poorly at the boxoffice, it ended his eleven-year association with the studio.

STARRING: Claudette Colbert, Gary Cooper, Edward Everett Horton, David Niven, Elizabeth Patterson
PRODUCER: Ernst Lubitsch
DIRECTOR: Ernst Lubitsch
SCREENPLAY: Charles Brackett, Billy Wilder
ADAPTATION: Charlton Andrews
PICTURED: *Gary Cooper, Claudette Colbert*

ADOLPH ZUKOR PRESENTS

CLAUDETTE COLBERT   GARY COOPER

with

EDWARD EVERETT HORTON

• DAVID NIVEN •

ELIZABETH PATTERSON

• HERMAN BING •

Produced and Directed by

ERNST LUBITSCH

Screen Play by Charles Brackett and Billy Wilder

Based on the Play by Alfred Savoir
English Play Adaptation by Charlton Andrews

A Paramount Picture

"BLUEBEARD'S EIGHTH WIFE"

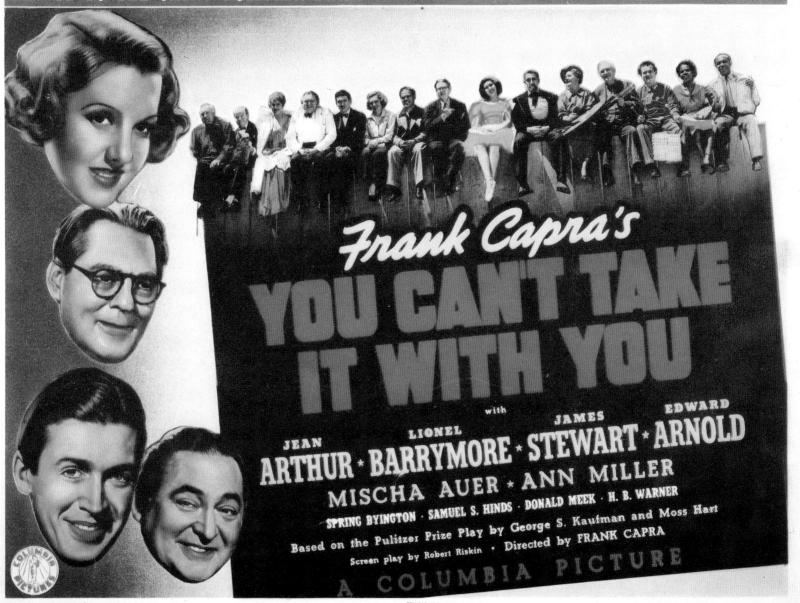

YOU CAN'T TAKE IT WITH YOU

1938 · Columbia

This movie adaptation of the Puliter Prize-winning play by Kaufman and Hart won the 1938 Oscar for Best Picture and Best Director and was nominated in five other categories. In Capra's version the daft Sycamore family makes multimillionaire financial wizard/munitions dealer Kirby (Arnold) — "Why, a war wouldn't be possible anywhere without us!" — a benign, happy-go-lucky fella. At the end of the film he is reunited with his son Tony (Stewart), who marries Alice Sycamore (Arthur). Blissfully eccentric, harmonica-playing Grandpa (Barrymore) is the patriarch of the family. He portrays the ubiquitous and prototypical Capra character who tells us that a man's wealth is determined by the number of his friends: Grandpa is supported in court by hundreds of friends while Kirby must rely on the well paid services of his four lawyers. Capra's empathy with the essential goodness of the poor, honest working man was described as Capra-corn by his detractors. Lionel Barrymore, using crutches in this film, shows the ravages of the crippling arthritis that hereafter kept him confined to a wheelchair on-and-off-screen.

STARRING: Jean Arthur, Lionel Barrymore, James Stewart, Edward Arnold, Mischa Auer, Ann Miller
PRODUCER: Frank Capra
DIRECTOR: Frank Capra
SCREENPLAY: Robert Riskin, based on the Pulitzer Prize-winning play by George S. Kaufman and Moss Hart
PICTURED: *Top to bottom, Jean Arthur, Lionel Barrymore, James Stewart, Edward Arnold. Seated in the middle on the fence, director Frank Capra.*

BRINGING UP BABY

1938 · RKO

An absentminded scientist-professor David Huxley (Grant) is the romantic objective of madcap heiress Susan (Hepburn). The antics of her pet leopard Baby and the family dog George combine with her well intentioned addlebrained scheming to make a shambles of his well ordered, unadventureous life. When David, a zoologist, is assembling a brontosaurus skeleton, George runs off with and buries the one crucial bone: the intercostal clavicle. Meanwhile Baby (who responds kindly only to "I Can't Give You Anything But Love....") wanders away and, in an unusual case of mistaken identity, is confused with an escaped killer leopard. The hectic, breathless pace of Susan's pursuit of David culminates in that transcendent moment when, tottering on the laboratory scaffolding in an attempt to reach her man, she destroys his precious assemblage of old bones. Surprisingly, this sparkling film was not a success when it was first released. Hepburn, whose film career was faltering and who had been declared "box-office poison," returned to the stage. She remained off-screen until 1940 when she reteamed with Grant in PHILADELPHIA STORY. Grant, who had previously co-starred with Hepburn in SYLVIA SCARLETT, was fourth in line for the role of Huxley — Ray Milland, Robert Montgomery and Ronald Colman had turned it down. Howard Hawks, the versatile director whose initial foray into comedy was TWENTIETH CENTURY, went on to direct many of the screen's finest screwball comedies, including HIS GIRL FRIDAY and BALL OF FIRE.

STARRING: Katharine Hepburn, Cary Grant, Charles Ruggles, Walter Catlett, May Robson
PRODUCER: Howard Hawks
DIRECTOR: Howard Hawks
ORIGINAL STORY: Hagar Wilde
SCREENPLAY: Dudley Nichols, Hagar Wilde
PICTURED: *Cary Grant, Katharine Hepburn*

Katharine
HEPBURN
CARY GRANT
in
A HOWARD HAWKS
PRODUCTION
Bringing Up Baby
COUNTRY OF ORIGIN U. S. A.

PARAMOUNT presents

CLAUDETTE COLBERT · DON AMECHE

MIDNIGHT

with **JOHN BARRYMORE** · **FRANCIS LEDERER** · **MARY ASTOR**

ELAINE BARRIE

Screen Play by Charles Brackett and Billy Wilder · Based on a story by Edwin Justus Mayer and Franz Schulz

Directed by Mitchell Leisen

A Paramount Picture

MIDNIGHT

1939 · Paramount

Leisen's comedy masterpiece presents a powerhouse cast in a sensational Brackett-Wilder script that bubbles with surprises. Eve Peabody (Colbert), a beautiful, young and penniless American girl, strikes a bargain with eccentric, aging aristocrat Flammarian (Barrymore). She will masquerade as his mistress, the "Countess Czerny," to arouse the jealousy of his wife (Astor) who is dallying with *bon vivant* Picot (Lederer). Picot finds himself attracted to Peabody, who leads him on as instructed by Flammarian. Peabody's fiancé (Ameche) arrives on the scene in the guise of her husband "Count Czerny" to claim her. As a wily, tough-talking gold digger, Colbert is first class as she party-crashes her way into swanky society. Former architect, costume designer and art director Leisen created a sumptuous setting for this sophisticated comedy. Wilder and Brackett's long and fruitful collaboration began in the late '30s with the witty screwball comedies BLUEBEARD'S EIGHTH WIFE, MIDNIGHT, NINOTCHKA and BALL OF FIRE, and culminated in their Oscar-winning screenplays for LOST WEEKEND (1945) and SUNSET BOULEVARD (1950).

STARRING: Claudette Colbert, Don Ameche, John Barrymore, Francis Lederer, Mary Astor
PRODUCER: Arthur Hornblow, Jr.
DIRECTOR: Mitchell Leisen
STORY: Franz Schulz and Edwin Justus Mayer
SCREENPLAY: Charles Brackett, Billy Wilder
PICTURED: *Frances Lederer, Don Ameche, Claudette Colbert, John Barrymore*

YOU CAN'T CHEAT AN HONEST MAN

1 9 3 9 · Universal

Fields, as the blustering side-show barker Whipsnade, trades insults throughout this hilarious, fast-paced circus comedy with his nemesis Charlie McCarthy — a feud that continued off-screen and onto the airwaves. Fields first introduced the character Larson E. Whipsnade to the CBS radio audience of "Your Hit Parade." Ventriloquist Bergen and his dummy McCarthy were radio personalities who had appeared in a dozen film shorts before finding immense popularity in features. In 1937 Bergen won a special Academy Award for his creation of Charlie McCarthy. This was Fields' first film for Universal, the studio that had lured him away from Paramount with an offer of $125,000 per film plus $25,000 for each story. He clashed with director Marshall, and Cline, who could weather Fields' abuse, was brought in to smoothe the comedian's ruffled feathers and direct his scenes.

STARRING: W. C. Fields, Edgar Bergen, Charlie McCarthy, Constance Moore
PRODUCER: Lester Cowan
DIRECTOR: George Marshall, Eddie Cline
ORIGINAL STORY: Charles Bogle (W. C. Fields)
SCREENPLAY: George Marion, Jr., Richard Mack, Everet Freeman
PICTURED: *W. C. Fields, Charlie McCarthy, Edgar Bergen*

W.C. FIELDS *You Can't Cheat an Honest Man* with Edgar BERGEN Charlie McCARTHY A NEW UNIVERSAL PICTURE

GRETA GARBO

"I love Russians! I have been fascinated by your Five Year Plan for 15 years!"

NINOTCHKA

A Metro-Goldwyn-Mayer Picture

COUNTRY OF ORIGIN U.S.A.

NINOTCHKA

1939 · MGM

From "Garbo Talks!" in ANNA CHRISTIE (1930) to "Garbo Laughs!" nine years later, playing a Soviet agent in Paris who falls for the dashing Count Leon D'Algout (Douglas). In her impressive introduction to screwball comedy, the classic, mysterious beauty is also funny. Garbo's dour, implacable Russian soldier utterly captivates the high-living boulevardier with her humorless, deadpan dogma. After countless silly jokes fail, Douglas finally makes her laugh when he tumbles off his chair in a restaurant. It's an endearing romance that unfolds with wit, intelligence and the Lubitsch appreciation of the complexities of human nature. It was Garbo's second-to-last film; two years later she bid adieu to her screen career with TWO-FACED WOMAN (1941). The debonair Douglas, "the man who made Garbo laugh," first starred with her in AS YOU DESIRE ME (1932), and was one of the most popular leading men of the '30s and '40s.

STARRING: Greta Garbo, Melvyn Douglas, Ina Claire, Sig Rumann, Felix Bressart, Alexander Granach
PRODUCER: Ernst Lubitsch
DIRECTOR: Ernst Lubitsch
SCREENPLAY: Charles Brackett, Billy Wilder, Walter Reisch; based on an original story by Melchior Lengyel
PICTURED: *Greta Garbo, Melvyn Douglas*

HIS GIRL FRIDAY

1940 · Columbia

After years of playing "the other woman" roles, Russell soared to stardom as reporter Hildy Johnson in Hawks' crackling version of the great Hecht-MacArthur newspaper comedy, THE FRONT PAGE. A Broadway hit in 1928, the stage play was first brought to the screen in 1931 by producer Howard Hughes with Lewis Milestone directing Pat O'Brien in the Hildy Johnson role. In a stroke of genius, Hawks conceived the idea of shaping the story around Johnson as a woman reporter, with her editor Walter Burns (Grant) not only her boss but her ex-husband and Bellamy stepping in as Bruce, her nicer-than-nice fiancé. Slam-bang, popcorn-popping spontaneity and a hard-edged sense of reality is Hawk's signature in screwball comedy-romance. Here in the tough, cynical world of the daily newspaper, the scoundrel editor attempts to win back his prize reporter and former wife by offering, "You can come back to work on the paper , and if we find we can't get along in a friendly fashion, we'll get married again." Improvisation, too, was a hallmark of Hawk's directing style and among Grant's ad libs is "The last person to say that to me was Archie Leach before he cut his throat." Archie Leach was Grant's real name.

STARRING: Cary Grant, Rosalind Russell, Ralph Bellamy, Gene Lockhart, Porter Hall
PRODUCER: Howard Hawks
DIRECTOR: Howard Hawks
SCREENPLAY: Charles Lederer, based on the play THE FRONT PAGE by Ben Hecht and Charles MacArthur
PICTURED: *Cary Grant, Rosalind Russell, Ralph Bellamy*

CARY
GRANT
ROSALIND
RUSSELL

A COLUMBIA PICTURE

Howard Hawks'
HIS GIRL FRIDAY

PRINTED IN U.S.A.

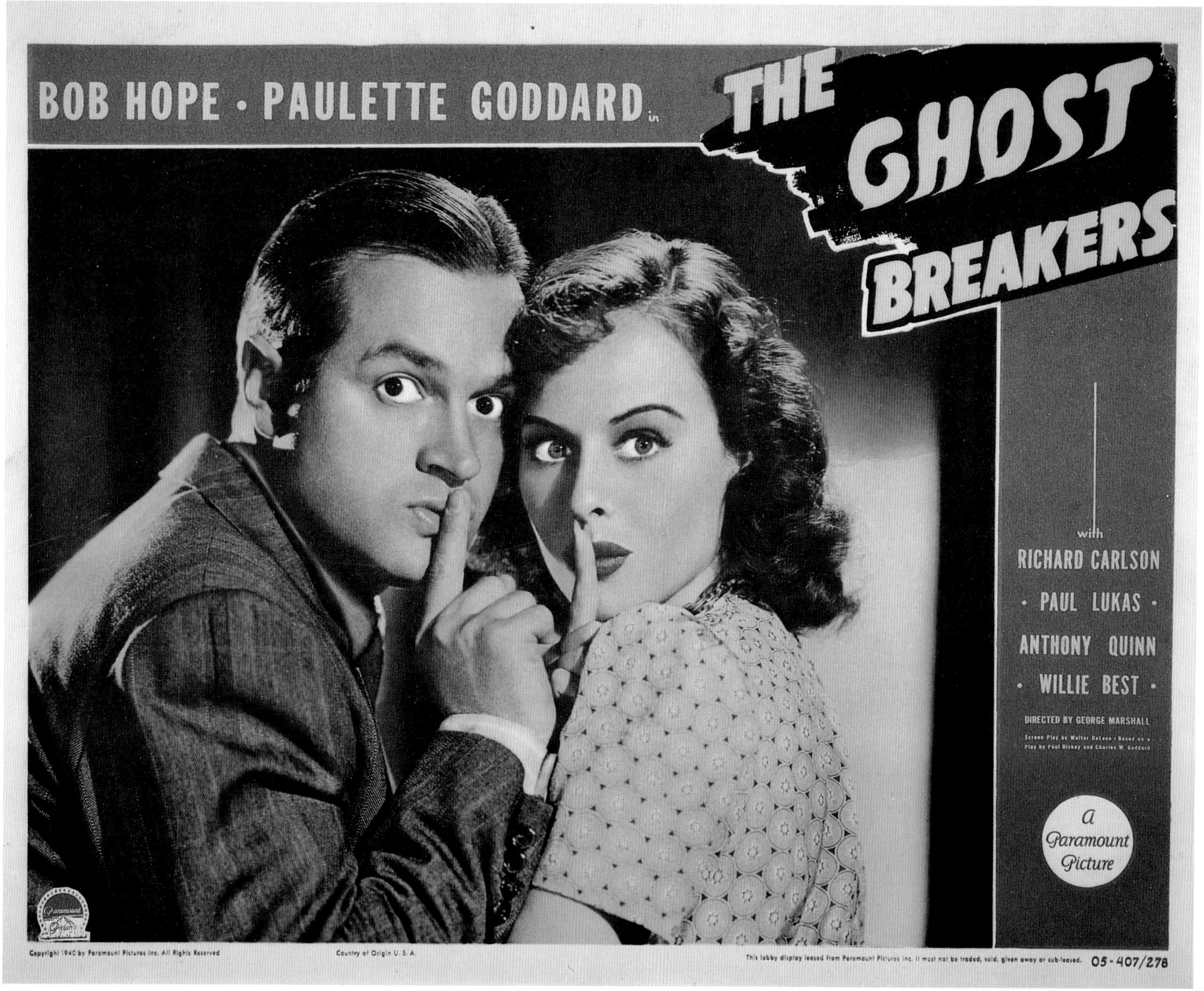

BOB HOPE · PAULETTE GODDARD in
THE GHOST BREAKERS
with
RICHARD CARLSON
· PAUL LUKAS ·
ANTHONY QUINN
· WILLIE BEST ·
DIRECTED BY GEORGE MARSHALL
Screen Play by Walter DeLeon · Based on a Play by Paul Dickey and Charles W. Goddard
A Paramount Picture
Copyright 1940 by Paramount Pictures Inc. All Rights Reserved
Country of Origin U. S. A.
This lobby display leased from Paramount Pictures Inc. It must not be traded, sold, given away or sub-leased.
05-407/278

THE GHOST BREAKERS

1940 · Paramount

Hope plays an amateur sleuth who stumbles through a farcical melodrama in a haunted castle in Cuba with its own resident zombie (Johnson). After their success in THE CAT AND THE CANARY, Hope and Goddard were reunited in this romantic-comedy adventure, and it was the best of their three films together. They subsequently teamed in NOTHING BUT THE TRUTH (1941). THE GHOST BREAKERS is also the best of the four versions of the story — filmed first in 1915 with H. B. Warner, remade in 1922 with Wallace Reid and again in 1953 as SCARED STIFF with Dean Martin and Jerry Lewis. George Marshall, who made six other films with Hope, also directed the Martin and Lewis version.

STARRING: Bob Hope, Paulette Goddard, Paul Lukas, Richard Carlson, Anthony Quinn, Noble Johnson
PRODUCER: Arthur Hornblow, Jr.
DIRECTOR: George Marshall
SCREENPLAY: Walter DeLeon
PICTURED: *Bob Hope, Paulette Goddard*

THE PHILADELPHIA STORY

1940 · MGM

Hepburn's comeback film was a huge success for all involved, and a personal triumph that rescued her career. Philip Barry's stylish play about a privileged society girl was written for Hepburn, who had spent two months working on the script with the writer, and it became a huge Broadway success. Hepburn, who owned twenty-three per cent of the play's stock, bought the screen rights from Barry and sold the package, with her choice of director (Cukor) and leading men (Grant as her ex-husband and Stewart as a smitten reporter) to MGM. Grant, who got top billing and his choice of roles, claimed that the film was one of his favorites. He donated his fee to the British War Relief. Stewart won the Academy Award for Best Actor, Donald Ogden Stewart won the Oscar for Best Screenplay, and the film was nominated in six categories altogether. Hepburn won the New York Film Critics' Award, a victory to savor after having been labeled "boxoffice poison" and "Katharine the Arrogant."

STARRING: Cary Grant, Katharine Hepburn, James Stewart, Ruth Hussey, John Howard, Roland Young
PRODUCER: Joseph L. Mankiewicz
DIRECTOR: George Cukor
SCREENPLAY: Donald Ogden Stewart, based on the play by Philip Barry
PICTURED: *Virginia Weidler, Mary Nash, Cary Grant, Katharine Hepburn*

Cary **GRANT**
Katharine **HEPBURN**
James **STEWART**
in
The Philadelphia Story

"You try to live like a prudish goddess! If only your
foot would slip some time...and hard!"

A Metro-Goldwyn-Mayer PICTURE

COUNTRY OF ORIGIN U. S. A.

UNIVERSAL PICTURES presents

W.C. FIELDS
in
THE
Bank Dick

THE BANK DICK

1940 · Universal

The town's foremost souse, bank guard Egbert Souse (pronounced soo-zay), inadvertantly becomes the local celebrity during an attempted robbery. Preferring the companionship of his drinking cronies at The Black Pussy saloon to life at home with his miserable family, Souse is an unlikely hero. In a hilarious spoof of the American dream, he cashes in on a $5,000 reward for capturing a bank robber, a $10,000 movie contract, and becomes part-owner of the fantastically rich Beefsteak Mines. This film and IT'S A GIFT are considered Field's masterpieces.

STARRING: W. C. Fields, Cora Witherspoon, Una Merkel, Franklin Pangborn, Jessie Ralph
DIRECTOR: Eddie Cline
SCREENPLAY: Mahatma Kane Jeeves (W. C. Fields)
PICTURED: *W. C. Fields, Franklin Pangborn*

THE GREAT DICTATOR

1940 · United Artists

"He talks..." In Chaplin's first all-talking film, he dared to take an early stand against Hitler and fascism, playing the dual role of a Jewish ghetto barber and Toumanian dictator Adenoid Hynkel, leader of the Double Cross Party. Chaplin's friends had urged him to do a satirical comedy about the impending war. At first he rejected the idea as too grim, then became intrigued with the possibilities as he watched newsreels of Hitler, declaring, "That guy's a great actor — the greatest actor of us all." Scotch-Irish Jack Oakie, persuaded to forgo his diet, was cast as Napolini of Bacteria, a combination Napoleon and Mussolini, with Chaplin's wife Paulette Goddard playing Hannah. Filming commenced September 9, 1939, a week after World War II erupted. Chaplin, who shot all of his scenes as the barber first, then those of the dictator, remarked that just putting on the uniform altered his personality and made him feel contemptuously superior. Deliriously intoxicated with his power, Hynkel, in one of Chaplin's most powerful metaphors, spins a world globe in his hands which becomes a balloon and his partner in a ballet. When it bursts, Hynkel sobs bitterly. The film opened in England at the height of the blitz and was a welcome morale booster. It's reception in America was mixed: a Gallup poll indicated that ninety-six per cent of the American people opposed entering the war. On the other hand, they regretted siding against their beloved little tramp. Chaplin was told on good authority that Nazi agents had secured a print for Hitler, who watched the film alone; Chaplin never learned what der Fuhrer thought of it.

STARRING: Charles Chaplin, Paulette Goddard, Jack Oakie, Henry Daniell, Reginald Gardiner
PRODUCER, DIRECTOR, WRITER: Charles Chaplin
PICTURED: *Paulette Goddard, Charles Chaplin, Jack Oakie*

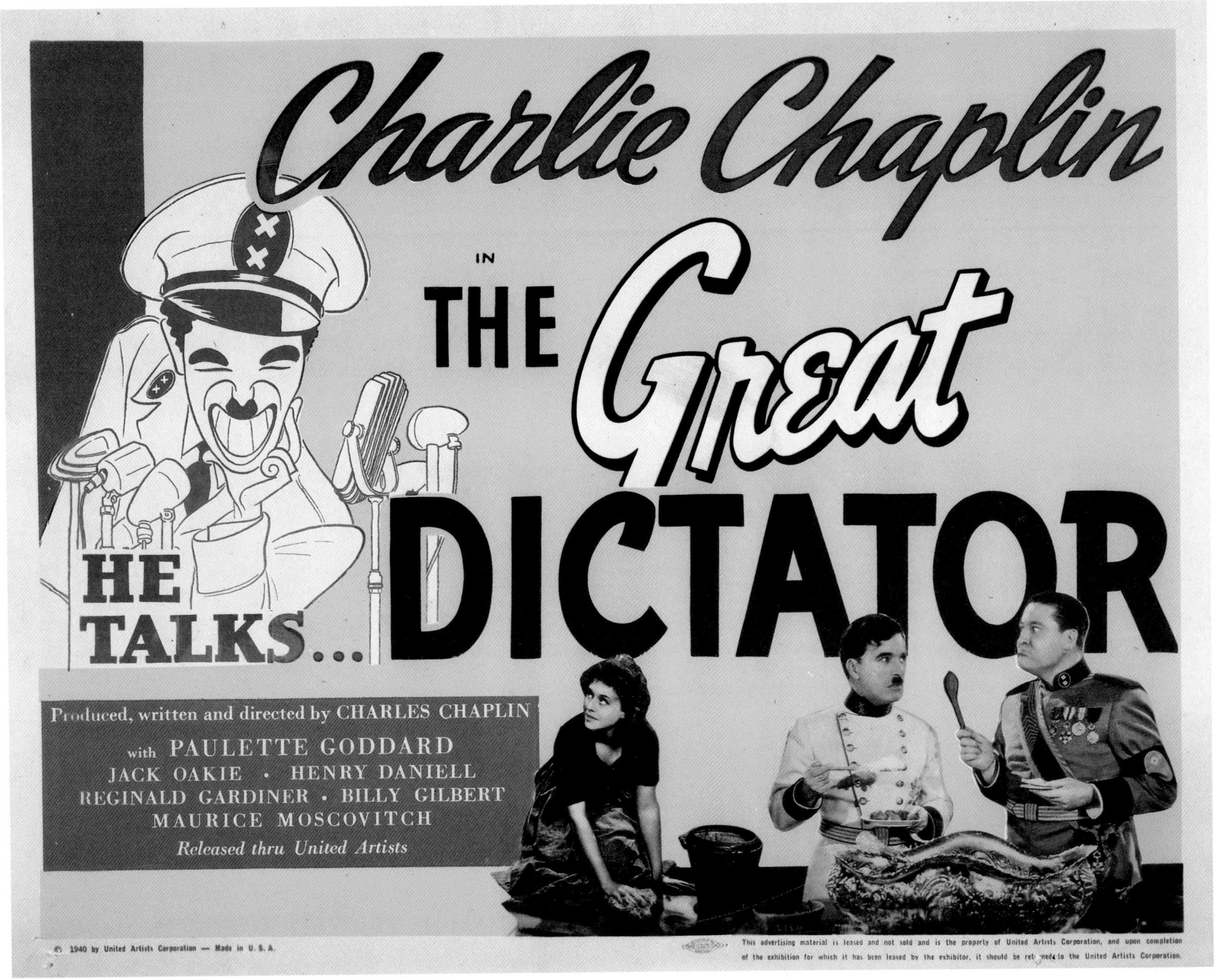

Charlie Chaplin
IN
THE Great DICTATOR
HE TALKS...
Produced, written and directed by CHARLES CHAPLIN
with PAULETTE GODDARD
JACK OAKIE · HENRY DANIELL
REGINALD GARDINER · BILLY GILBERT
MAURICE MOSCOVITCH
Released thru United Artists
© 1940 by United Artists Corporation — Made in U. S. A.
This advertising material is leased and not sold and is the property of United Artists Corporation, and upon completion of the exhibition for which it has been leased by the exhibitor, it should be returned to the United Artists Corporation.

Bette **DAVIS** Ann **SHERIDAN** Monty **WOOLLEY**

"The Man Who Came to Dinner"

Country of Origin U. S. A.

THE MAN WHO CAME TO DINNER

1941 · Warner Bros.

On a lecture engagement, pompous, demanding critic Sheridan Whiteside (Woolley) is injured while a guest of the Burke's, forcing him and his mousy but strong-willed secretary (Davis) to remain in the family home for the winter. Whiteside's motley assortment of witty, sophisticated and self-centered friends descend on the small town family bringing with them their highly theatrical screwball romances, jealousies and business affairs. A major hit for Warner's, this film provided Davis and Ann Sheridan with showy roles as rivals for the same man, and helped elevate former supporting player Woolley to a brief run of stardom during the war years. Davis had wanted John Barrymore for the Whiteside character, but the actor had to forfeit the role because he could no longer remember his lines. This was one of Ann Sheridan's five films in 1941, including KING'S ROW and GEORGE WASHINGTON SLEPT HERE. The Epstein brothers collaborated on many screenplays, sharing the 1943 Academy Award for CASABLANCA.

STARRING: Bette Davis, Ann Sheridan, Monty Woolley, Richard Travis, Jimmy Durante
EXECUTIVE PRODUCER: Hal B. Wallis
ASSOCIATE PRODUCER: Jack Saper, Jerry Wald
DIRECTOR: William Keighley
SCREENPLAY: Julius J. and Philip G. Epstein, based on the play by George S. Kaufman and Moss Hart
PICTURED: *Monty Woolley, Bette Davis, Ann Sheridan*

THE ROAD TO ZANZIBAR

1941 · Paramount

This film was based on a serious dramatic tale by Sy Bartlett called FIND COLONEL FAWCETT; about two men lost in the tangled jungles of Madagascar, it paralleled the real-life Stanley and Livingston story. Butler and Hartman used the story to craft a spoof of musical jungle pictures, which Hope and Crosby instilled with their own brand of freewheeling ad libs. It's well known that they didn't stick to the scripts — at times Hope delivered his off-the-cuff asides directly to the camera — and that their clowning disturbed mild-mannered director Schertzinger. However, the film won praise from the critics and was a boxoffice smash. This picture firmly established the style evident in all seven Crosby-Hope "road" pictures: zany, nonsensical adventures with musical interludes set in exotic locales featuring the wisecracking duo and the object of their romantic desires, Lamour, in comic peril.

STARRING: Bing Crosby, Bob Hope, Dorothy Lamour, Una Merkel, Eric Blore
PRODUCER: Paul Jones
DIRECTOR: Victor Schertzinger
SCREENPLAY: Frank Butler, Don Hartman
PICTURED: *Bing Crosby, Bob Hope*

BING
CROSBY

BOB
HOPE

DOROTHY
LAMOUR

A
PARAMOUNT
PICTURE

IN
ROAD TO ZANZIBAR

WITH UNA MERKEL · ERIC BLORE

Directed by Victor Schertzinger
Screen Play by Frank Butler and Don Hartman

414/93

BING CROSBY
BOB HOPE
DOROTHY LAMOUR

A PARAMOUNT PICTURE

IN **ROAD TO MOROCCO**

ANTHONY QUINN
DONA DRAKE
Directed by DAVID BUTLER
Original Screen Play by Frank Butler and Don Hartman

THE ROAD TO MOROCCO

1942 · Paramount

This spoof of desert epics opens with Hope and Crosby perched on camels singing the title song which includes the lyric "...I'll lay you eight to five we meet Dorothy Lamour." They do, and Anthony Quinn, playing a desert prince, is her betrothed. In the classic teaming, Hope is always the butt of the joke; his cowardly, egotistical, ever romantic character always loses the girl to the cool, suave Crosby.

STARRING: Bing Crosby, Bob Hope, Dorothy Lamour, Anthony Quinn, Dona Drake
ASSOCIATE PRODUCER: Paul Jones
DIRECTOR: David Butler
SCREENPLAY: Frank Butler, Don Hartman
MUSIC: James Van Heusen & Johnny Burke
PICTURED: *Bob Hope, Dona Drake, Dorothy Lamour, Bing Crosby*

BUCK PRIVATES

1941 · Universal

This was a pivotal picture for Abbott and Costello who first teamed for comedy sketches in a Brooklyn theatre in 1931. Their boxoffice success in this feature assured them of a devoted movie audience throughout the '40s in a series of loosely constructed comedy films that accomodated their well worked, fast talking burlesque routines. Tall, good-looking straightman Abbott and short, pudgy funnyman Costello were a top boxoffice attraction, particularly through the war years, and "Boogie Woogie Bugle Boy," one of the Andrews Sisters' songs, became a wartime classic.

STARRING: Lee Bowman, Alan Curtis, Bud Abbott, Lou Costello, the Andrews Sisters
PRODUCER: Alex Gottlieb
DIRECTOR: Arthur Lubin
SCREENPLAY: Arthur T. Horman
PICTURED: *Bud Abbott, Shemp Howard, Lou Costello*

BUD ABBOTT and LOU COSTELLO in

UNIVERSAL

BUCK PRIVATES

A UNIVERSAL PICTURE

Copyright 1941 Universal Pictures Company, Inc. — Country of Origin U.S.A.

BUD
ABBOTT · COSTELLO
in
HOLD THAT
GHOST

LOU

A UNIVERSAL PICTURE

Copyright 1941 Universal Pictures Company, Inc. — Country of Origin U.S.A.

HOLD THAT GHOST

1941 · Universal

Abbott and Costello's fourth movie was filmed prior to the general release of BUCK PRIVATES. Because of the latter film's tremendous success, musical sequences with Ted Lewis and the Andrews Sisters were added to increase the GHOST's boxoffice appeal. This was actor-turned-director Lubin's third picture with Abbott and Costello; Lubin was later to find questionable fame directing the Francis, the Talking Mule series at Universal. Joan (christened Madonna) Davis, the Minnesota born slapstick comedienne, had teamed with husband Sy Wills in the Wills and Davis vaudeville act. When she moved into films, she was most often cast as the goofy, man-hungry spinster and, in her raucous knockabout style, she often slugged herself in the jaw for dizzy-dame comic effect. She later found great popularity as star of her own television comedy series "I Married Joan" as the wife of Jim Backus.

STARRING: Bud Abbott, Lou Costello, Richard Carlson, Evelyn Ankers, Joan Davis
PRODUCER: Burt Kelly, Glenn Tryon
DIRECTOR: Arthur Lubin
SCREENPLAY: Robert Lees, Fred Rinaldo, John Grant
PICTURED: *Lou Costello, Bud Abbott, Joan Davis*

TO BE OR NOT TO BE

1942 · United Artists

A fitting capstone to a sparkling film career, Lombard's last film was released within two months of her tragic death in an airplane crash. Her fine comic skills were showcased in this melding of comedy and drama dealing with the Nazi invasion of Poland. As Lombard's husband, Benny appears in his best screen role playing a Shakespearean actor who, when his Polish theatre troupe disbands, finds himself involved in espionage posing as a well known Gestapo spy. For the Berlin-born Lubitsch (once a young actor with Max Reinhardt's company) this anti-Nazi film was a very personal project, for which he engaged CHILDREN OF DARKNESS playwright Edwin Justus Mayer as screenwriter. By the time filming was completed America had entered the war, and many viewers were appalled by a comedy based on fascism. Faced with the grim reality of war in the daily newspaper, audiences were unprepared for the light hearted comic treatment of Nazis as movie entertainment.

STARRING: Carole Lombard, Jack Benny, Robert Stack, Felix Bressart, Lionel Atwill
PRODUCER: Ernst Lubitsch
DIRECTOR: Ernst Lubitsch
ORIGINAL STORY: Melchior Lengyel
SCREENPLAY: Edwin Justus Mayer
PICTURED: *Carole Lombard, Jack Benny*

The Picture Everyone Wants to See
Alexander KORDA presents
Carole Lombard
Jack Benny
in Ernst LUBITSCH'S
COMEDY
TO BE or NOT to BE
WITH
ROBERT STACK · FELIX BRESSART · LIONEL ATWILL
STANLEY RIDGES · SIG RUMAN
Produced and directed by Ernst Lubitsch . . . Original story by Ernst Lubitsch and Melchior Lengyel . . . Screen play by Edwin Justus Mayer
RELEASED THRU UNITED ARTISTS
This advertising material is leased and not sold and is the property of United Artists Corporation, and upon completion of the exhibition for which it has been leased by the exhibitor, it should be returned to the United Artists Corporation.
© 1942 by United Artists Corporation—Made in U.S.A

HELLZAPOPPIN'
starring
OLSEN and JOHNSON
with
MARTHA RAYE
HUGH HERBERT MISCHA AUER
JANE FRAZEE ROBERT PAIGE
30 CONGEROOS
A UNIVERSAL PICTURE
UNIVERSAL
Copyright 1941 Universal Pictures Company, Inc. — Country of Origin U. S. A.

HELLZAPOPPIN'

1942 · Universal

Comedian Olsen and former ragtime pianist Johnson teamed in 1914 to become a popular vaudeville act. They made a number of films, but this fast paced, almost surrealist version of their Broadway hit was their most successful picture. Raye began her career as a child performing in her parents' vaudeville act and broke into films as a boisterous singer-comedienne.

STARRING: Ole Olsen, Chic Johnson, Martha Raye, Hugh Herbert, Mischa Auer
PRODUCERS: Glenn Tryon, Alex Gottlieb
DIRECTOR: H.C. Potter
SCREENPLAY: Nat Perrin and Warren Wilson, based on an original story by Nat Perrin
PICTURED: *Hugh Herbert, Mischa Auer, Ole Olsen, Chic Johnson, Martha Raye*

THE MIRACLE OF MORGAN'S CREEK

1944 · Paramount

In this wild, daring wartime farce, Trudy Kockenlocker (Hutton) attends a party, becomes pregnant by a soldier (whom she can't remember meeting) and gives birth to sextuplets. Not only did the family name get past the strict Production Code but also the sexual promiscuity at the heart of the plot, involving soldiers and hometown girls in wartime; as James Agee put it, "The Hays Office has been raped in its sleep." Sturges heyday as a director was brief and meteoric; in his four years at Paramount, he produced eight brilliant comedies and was reckoned a genius. Prior to directing his first film at age 42, the wealthy, European-educated Sturges had been an inventor — developing a kissproof lipstick for the family cosmetics firm — an Air Corps pilot and playwright-turned-screenwriter. Though his films were critical and boxoffice hits, and despite his acclaim on the Paramount lot for shooting long, complicated scenes in a single take, there was front-office interference that forced Sturges to leave the studio. Howard Hughes, another pilot/inventor, set Sturges up with his own studio — a disastrous venture. Finally he had a brief and unsatisfactory association with Darryl Zanuck at Twentieth Century-Fox. Sturges' rich legacy of brilliant, eccentric, outrageously funny comedies continue to inspire filmmakers. Never able to regain his '40s brilliance, he died of a heart attack in 1959. In Katharine Hepburn's estimation, he died of neglect.

STARRING: Eddie Bracken, Betty Hutton, William Demarest, Diana Lynn, Porter Hall
PRODUCER, DIRECTOR, WRITER: Preston Sturges
PICTURED: *Betty Hutton, William Demarest, Eddie Bracken, Diana Lynn*

The Miracle of Morgan's Creek

Starring **EDDIE BRACKEN** · **BETTY HUTTON**

with **DIANA LYNN** · **WILLIAM DEMAREST** · **PORTER HALL** and "McGINTY" and "The BOSS"

Written and Directed by **PRESTON STURGES** · A Paramount Picture

43/479

CARY GRANT in "ARSENIC and OLD LACE"

PRESENTED BY WARNER BROS

ARSENIC AND OLD LACE

1944 · Warner Bros.

The producers of Kesselring's Broadway hit — about two dotty, seemingly harmless Brooklyn spinsters who murder their gentlemen callers — stipulated that the film version couldn't be released until the play closed. The play ran for more than 1,300 performances. Because Jack Warner agreed to the terms, the picture that Capra quickly filmed in six weeks (in 1941) was finally released three years later. Capra had volunteered for the US Army Signal Corps, and wartime economies and pressures necessitated a speedy production. Three of the Broadway cast (Hull, Adair, Alexander) repeated their stage roles in the film during their four-week vacation. Karloff stayed with the play in New York because he was a major audience draw. Bob Hope turned down the role that Grant later accepted, and Grant reportedly donated his salary to War Relief.

STARRING: Cary Grant, Priscilla Lane, Peter Lorre, Raymond Massey, Josephine Hull, Jean Adair, Jack Carson, Edward Everett Horton
PRODUCER, DIRECTOR: Frank Capra
SCREENPLAY: Julius J. Epstein and Philip G. Epstein, based on the play by Joseph Kesselring
PICTURED: *Raymond Massey, Cary Grant, Peter Lorre*

THE SECRET LIFE OF WALTER MITTY

1947 · RKO

Thurber's quintessential milquetoast daydreamer (Kaye), who fancies himself in a succession of heroic roles, rescues Mayo from the clutches of a gang of jewel thieves. This boxoffice smash — in which he impersonates, among others, a surgeon, a cowboy and a pilot — was one of Kaye's best films and utilized his many talents. The singer-dancer-actor entered show business as a teenager in the Catskill Mountains' Borscht Circuit as a clowning waiter, then worked for years in nightclubs and vaudeville before achieving success on Broadway. His famous show-stopper was "Tchaikovsky," a musical number in which he reeled off the names of 54 Russian composers in 38 seconds.

STARRING: Danny Kaye, Virginia Mayo, Boris Karloff, Fay Bainter, Ann Rutherford
PRODUCER: Samuel Goldwyn
DIRECTOR: Norman Z. McLeod
SCREENPLAY: Ken Englund and Everett Freeman, based on the short story by James Thurber
PICTURED: *Virginia Mayo, Danny Kaye, Boris Karloff*

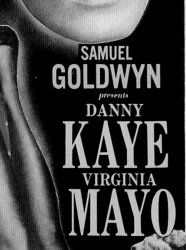

SAMUEL
GOLDWYN
presents
DANNY
KAYE
VIRGINIA
MAYO

in *The Secret Life of Walter Mitty*

in TECHNICOLOR

Released Through RKO Radio Pictures, Inc.

8

47/478

JEEPERS!
the CREEPERS are after BUD & LOU!!

UNIVERSAL INTERNATIONAL presents

BUD &
ABBOTT & COSTELLO LOU
meet
FRANKENSTEIN

with

The Wolfman PLAYED BY LON CHANEY
Dracula PLAYED BY BELA LUGOSI
The Monster PLAYED BY GLENN STRANGE

LENORE AUBERT · JANE RANDOLPH

Original Screenplay by Robert Lees · Frederic I. Rinaldo · John Grant

Directed by CHARLES T. BARTON
Produced by ROBERT ARTHUR

ABBOTT AND COSTELLO MEET FRANKENSTEIN

1948 · Universal

With too few hits and too many misses, Abbott and Costello needed a boxoffice success to boost their sagging careers in the late '40s, and they found it with the first of their "meet" movies. Later they were to meet onscreen with the Killer Boris Karloff (1949), the Invisible Man (1951), Captain Kidd (1952), Dr. Jekyll and Mr. Hyde (1953), the Keystone Kops (1955), and the Mummy (1955). The formula worked because the horror elements were played straight and the comedy arose out of the team's entanglements with the monsters. Vincent Price is heard but not seen at the end of this film as the Invisible Man. After more than 30 films together, Abbott and Costello broke up in 1957. Their most famous routine, "Who's on First?," is enshrined on a plaque in baseball's Hall of Fame.

STARRING: Bud Abbott, Lou Costello, Bela Lugosi, Lon Chaney, Jr., Glenn Strange, Lenore Aubert, Jane Randolph
PRODUCER: Robert Arthur
DIRECTOR: Charles Barton
SCREENPLAY: Robert Lees, Frederic I. Rinaldo, John Grant
PICTURED: *Bud Abbott, Bela Lugosi, Lon Chaney, Jr., Glenn Strange, Lou Costello*

A SOUTHERN YANKEE

1948 · MGM

With Buster Keaton on board as gag consultant and veteran comedy-hand Sedgwick directing, Skelton finally had a starring vehicle worthy of his talents. Set during the Civil War, this film presents Skelton as a bumbling Yankee spy in Confederate territory. Keaton devised the gag in which Skelton wins enthusiastic cheers from both Grays and the Blues by walking between the two warring camps wearing half of each army's uniform, each side seeing only their half. Skelton's flag was the Confederate and Union Jack sewn together. After a successful screen career, Skelton brought his superb slapstick and pantomime skills to television audiences, introducing them to Freddie the Freeloader and Clem Kadiddlehopper.

STARRING: Red Skelton, Brian Donlevy, Arlene Dahl, George Coulouris
PRODUCER: Paul Jones
DIRECTOR: Edward Sedgwick
SCREENPLAY: Harry Tugend, from an original story by Melvin Frank and Norman Panama
PICTURED: *Red Skelton, Arlene Dahl*

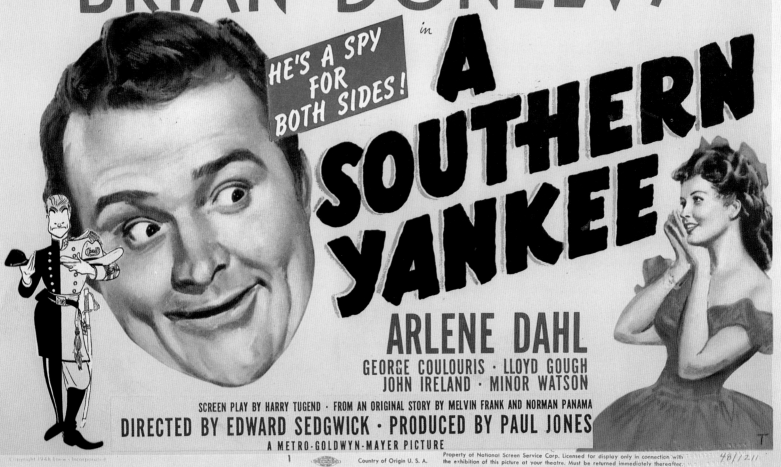

THE FUNNIEST PICTURE IN TEN YEARS!

SPENCER TRACY

KATHARINE HEPBURN

IT'S THE HILARIOUS ANSWER TO WHO WEARS THE PANTS!

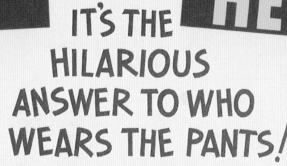

M-G-M's *Adam's Rib*

JUDY HOLLIDAY · TOM EWELL · DAVID WAYNE · JEAN HAGEN

Screen play by RUTH GORDON and GARSON KANIN · Directed by GEORGE CUKOR · Produced by LAWRENCE WEINGARTEN

A METRO-GOLDWYN-MAYER PICTURE

ADAM'S RIB

1949 · MGM

In this stylish, witty comedy, Adam (Tracy) and Amanda (Hepburn) are married lawyers pitted against each other in a court case. In their sixth teaming, Tracy and Hepburn are as cozy and comfortable together as a favorite pair of slippers that are still determined to be a right and a left. Former MGM comedienne Polly Moran returned to films for a brief cameo in the trial sequence after nearly a decade offscreen. As the birdbrained attempted murder suspect, Judy Holliday all but stole the picture; as a result, she was given the opportunity to reprise her Broadway role in BORN YESTER-DAY under Cukor's direction at Columbia Studios the following year — and won an Academy Award. The excellent supporting players were all Broadway actors. Hagen and Ewell (Holliday's victim) made their screen debuts in this film and Wayne made his initial screen appearance a year earlier in PORTRAIT OF JENNIE (1948).

STARRING: Spencer Tracy, Katharine Hepburn, Judy Holliday, Tom Ewell, David Wayne, Jean Hagen
PRODUCER: Lawrence Weingarten
DIRECTOR: George Cukor
PICTURED: *Spencer Tracy, Katharine Hepburn*

BIBLIOGRAPHY

THE AMAZING CAREERS OF BOB HOPE: FROM GAGS TO RICHES, by Joe Morella, Edward Z. Epstein and Eleanor Clark, Arlington House, 1973

AMERICAN SILENT FILM by William K. Everson, Oxford University Press, 1978

THE ART OF W.C. FIELDS by William K. Everson, The Bobbs-Merrill Co., Inc., 1967

BOB HOPE: PORTRAIT OF A SUPERSTAR, by Charles Thompson, St. Martin's Press, 1981

CARY GRANT: A CELEBRATION, by Richard Schickel, Little, Brown & Co., 1983

CARY GRANT: THE LIGHT TOUCH, by Lionel Godfrey, St. Martin's Press, 1981

CHAPLIN: HIS LIFE AND ART, by David Robinson; McGraw Hill Book Company, 1985

CHAPLIN: THE IMMORTAL TRAMP, by R. J. Minney, George Newnes Limited, 1954

CHARLES LAUGHTON: A DIFFICULT ACTOR, by Simon Callow, Methuen, London, 1987

CHARLIE CHAPLIN, by John McCabe, Doubleday & Company, 1978

CLOWN PRINCES AND COURT JESTERS, by Kalton C. Lahue and Samuel Gill, A. S. Barnes and Co., Inc., 1970

THE COMIC MIND: COMEDY AND THE MOVIES, by Gerald Mast, The Bobbs-Merrill Company, Inc., 1973

THE COMPLETE FILMS OF WILLIAM POWELL by Lawrence J. Quirk, The Citadel Press, 1986

THE DAY THE LAUGHTER STOPPED: THE TRUE STORY OF FATTY ARBUCKLE, by David A. Yallop, St. Martin's Press, 1976

DICTIONARY OF FILMMAKERS, by Georges Sadoul, Translated, Edited and Updated by Peter Morris, University of California Press, 1972

DICTIONARY OF FILMS, by Georges Sadoul, Translated, Edited and Updated by Peter Morris, University of California Press, 1972

EARLY AMERICAN CINEMA, Anthony Slide, with the assistance of Paul O'Dell; A. S. Barnes & Co., New York; A. Zwemmer Limited, London, 1970

EVERYBODY'S MAN: A BIOGRAPHY OF JAMES STEWART by Jan Robbins, G.P. Putnam's Sons, 1985

THE FILM ENCYCLOPEDIA by Ephraim Katz, The Putnam Publishing Group, 1979

THE FILMS OF CAROLE LOMBARD by Frederick W. Ott, The Citadel Press 1972

THE FILMS OF CARY GRANT by Donald Deschner, Citadel Press, 1973

THE FILMS OF JAMES STEWART by Ken D. Jones, Arthur F. McClure and Alfred E. Twombley, A. S. Barnes & Co., 1970

THE FILMS OF LAUREL & HARDY by William Everson, The Citadel Press, 1967

GENTLEMAN: THE WILLIAM POWELL STORY by Charles Francico, St. Martin's Press, 1985

THE GREAT MOVIE COMEDIANS, by Leonard Maltin; Crown Publishers, Inc., 1978

GROUCHO AND ME, by Groucho Marx, Bernard Geis Associates, 1959

HAROLD LLOYD: THE KING OF DAREDEVIL COMEDY by Adam Reilly, McMillan Publishing Co., 1977

HAROLD LLOYD: THE MAN ON THE CLOCK, by Tom Dardis; The Viking Press, 1983

HAROLD LLOYD: THE SHAPE OF LAUGHTER by Richard Schickel, New York Graphic Society, 1974

HAVE TUX, WILL TRAVEL: BOB HOPE'S OWN STORY AS TOLD TO PETE MARTIN, Simon and Schuster, 1954

HELLO, I MUST BE GOING: GROUCHO AND HIS FRIENDS by Charlotte Chandler, Doubleday & Co., 1978

HOLLYWOOD IN THE THIRTIES, John Baxter; A. Zwemmer Limited, London/A. S. Barnes & Co., New York; 1968

I OWE RUSSIA $1200, by Bob Hope, Doubleday & Company, Inc., 1963

KATHARINE: THE FILMS OF KATHARINE HEPBURN by Homer Dickens, The Citadel Press, 1971

KATHARINE HEPBURN by Sheridan Morley, Little, Brown & Co. 1984

KEATON, by Rudi Blesh; Collier Books, 1966

THE LAST CHRISTMAS SHOW, by Bob Hope as told to Pete Martin, Doubleday & Company, Inc. 1974

LAUREL AND HARDY: CLOWN PRINCES OF COMEDY, by Bruce Crowther, Columbus Books, London, 1987

LAUREL AND HARDY: THE MAGIC BEHIND THE MOVIES, by Randy Skretvedt, Moonstone Press, 1987

LE REGARD DO BUSTER KEATON by Robert Benayoun, Herscher, Paris, 1982

LEONARD MALTIN'S TV MOVIES AND VIDEO GUIDE 1987 EDITION, Edited by Leonard Maltin, New American Library, 1987

THE MARX BROTHERS AT THE MOVIES, by Paul D. Zimmerman and Burt Goldblatt; A Berkley Windhover Book, c. 1968

MOVIES OF THE SILENT YEARS by Ann Lloyd, Orbis Publishing, 1984

MOVIES OF THE THIRTIES by Ann Lloyd, Orbis Publishing, 1983

OUR GANG: THE LIFE AND TIMES OF THE LITTLE RASCALS, by Leonard Maltin and Richard W. Bann, Crown Publishers, Inc., 1977

A PICTORIAL HISTORY OF THE GREAT COMEDIANS, by William Cahn, Grosset & Dunlap, Inc., 1957

ROMANTIC COMEDY IN HOLLYWOOD, FROM LUBITSCH TO STURGES, by James Harvey, Alfred A. Knopf, 1987

SCREWBALL COMEDY: A GENRE OF MADCAP ROMANCE, by Wes D. Gehring, Greenwood Press, 1986

SCREWBALL: THE LIFE OF CAROLE LOMBARD by Larry Swindell, William Morrow & Co., 1975

THE SILENT CLOWNS by Walter Kerr, Alfred A. Knopf 1975

STAN: THE LIFE OF STAN LAUREL, by Fred Lawrence Guiles

TV, MOVIES AND VIDEO GUIDE (1987 EDITIONS) by Leonard Maltin, New American Library, 1986

TAKE MY LIFE, by Eddie Cantor with Jane Kesner Ardmore, Doubleday & Company, Inc., 1957.

THE THREE STOOGES SCRAPBOOK, by Jeff Lenburg, Joan Howard Maurer and Greg Lenberg, Citadel Press, 1982

W.C. FIELDS: A BIO-BIBLIOGRAPHY, by Wes D. Gehring, Greenwood Press, 1984

WOMEN IN COMEDY, by Linda Martin and Kerry Segrave, Citadel Press, 1986

WORLD OF LAUGHTER: THE MOTION PICTURE COMEDY SHORT, 1910 - 1930, by Kalton C. Lahue, University of Oklahoma Press, 1966

YESTERDAY'S CLOWNS: THE RISE OF FILM COMEDY, by Frank Manchel; Franklin Watts, Inc., 1973

INDEX